Lifelong
Landscape Design

Lifelong Landscape Design

Mary Palmer Dargan, ASLA

GIBBS SMITH
TO ENR CH AND INSPIRE HUMANKIND

PREVIOUS OVERLEAF: This elegant New Orleans garden, home to Jennifer and Fred Heebe, sports a bluestone terrace and custom-made furniture designed by the author and produced by Kenneth Lynch and Sons in Connecticut.

FACING: Oscar, the French bulldog, looks on with envy as Huckleberry, the mixed terrier, scampers across the stepping-stone pond, "Lake Charles."

PAGE 6: The Dargans enjoy al fresco meals by the lake at Highcote, their home in High Hampton, Cashiers, North Carolina, a lifelong project that keeps them close to nature.

First Edition
16 15 14 13 12   5 4 3 2 1
Text and photographs © 2012 Mary Palmer Dargan

Published by
Gibbs Smith
P.O. Box 667
Layton, Utah 84041

1.800.835.4993 orders
www.gibbs-smith.com

Designed by Debra McQuiston
Printed and bound in China

Gibbs Smith books are printed on either recycled, 100% post-consumer waste, FSC-certified papers or on paper produced from sustainable PEFC-certified forest/controlled wood source. Learn more at www.pefc.org.

Library of Congress Cataloging-in-Publication Data

Dargan, Mary Palmer.
  Lifelong landscape design / Mary Palmer Dargan. — 1st ed.
      p. cm.
  Includes bibliographical references and index.
  ISBN 978-1-4236-2072-3
1. Landscape design. 2. Landscape architecture. I. Title.
  SB472.45.D36 2012
  712—dc23
                          2012006755

Contents

ACKNOWLEDGMENTS

ABOVE: Holicot in Cashiers features a "walkable" path disguised to slow you down to smell the roses.

RIGHT: The end of the "snail's trail" at Timberline terminates under the dining table on the upper terrace.

To writers of so many books read during research, I cannot thank you enough for your inspired works and the influence it had on the depth of this design book. You walk with me on a daily basis.

My coauthor—partner in all aspects of life from gardening and hiking, to the office, in addition to being the best activities model for book photographs—is Hugh Graham Dargan, ASLA. He deserves a high sign of love and thanks, and much more than a kiss and a casserole. Since I seem to be living between the pages of this book, he wanted me to put my name on it, but it could never have been written without him.

The creative professionals at Dargan Landscape Architects who took rough sketches and made them into measured drawings or found ancient plans in our database are Becky Hillis, Curt Jackson and Corey Watson. I know it was in the line of duty, but your enthusiasm for this book is very supportive.

My publishers, especially Madge Baird, the senior editor who encouraged me to cut about 15,000 words, I appreciate your craft and suggestions. To Hollie Keith, now my senior editor, for shoehorning so much data between the pages of this book. To Christopher Robbins from Gibbs Smith who called the day after I'd written an outline and put it into a file folder entitled "Next Book!?," asking if I had ideas for another book. . . . Well, synchrodestiny?

Architects John Isch, Norman Akins, Martin Shofner and the late James R. Cothran, FASLA, for their contributions to dwelling styles and mentorship.

Jo Tunstall, expert editor from *National Geographic,* who read the introduction and provided insight while on vacation at my home. Mary-Kate Mackey, editor extraordinaire at University of Oregon, reached out to me after a transitions workshop at an annual garden writers conference and said, "I would love to read your manuscript."

Professional photographers suggested many things for which I am thankful. Even though I've practiced and honed my photography for fifty years, transitioning the digital age from my Hassle-blad to a far lighter Lumex Panasonic proves that even an old dog can learn new tricks. Just adjusting the diopter on a new digital camera made a world of difference, thank you Joseph DeSciose.

Garden owners, this book would not be here without you:

Jennifer and Fred Heebe, New Orleans, LA
Susan and Charles Reeder, High Hampton, NC
Highcote, High Hampton, NC
Linda and Dick Cravey, Cashiers, NC
Lana and Tommy Valenta, Cashiers, NC
Susan and John Akitt, Cashiers, NC
Nola and Charles Falcone, Augusta, GA
Judy and George Dixon, Cashiers, NC
Gail and Robert O'Leary, Atlanta, GA
Joyce Kilmer Memorial Forest, Robbinsville, NC
Kate and Bruce Knauft, Atlanta, GA
Lucy and Jack Kuhne, Highlands, NC
Asheville Arboretum, Asheville, NC
Balsam Mountain Preserve, Waynesville, NC
Justice and Mrs. George Peagler, Americus, GA

John and Billings Cay, Cashiers, NC
Cornelia and Tom Richards, Cashiers, NC
Heale House, England
Cristine Cozzins and Ron Calabrese, Atlanta, GA
Corabel and Martin Shofner, Cashiers, NC
Julie and Bill Baxter, Las Vegas, NV
Kristen and David Griffin, Oklahoma City, OK
Kayrita and Harold Anderson, Atlanta, GA
Susan and Bill Young, Glenville, NC
Margaret and Warren Wills, Atlanta, GA, and Cashiers, NC
Kreiss and Sandy Beall, Blackberry Farm, Wayland, TN
Highlands Country Club, Highlands, NC
Gerard McCann, Atlanta, GA
Barbara Graham, Columbia, SC
Mary and Rick Inman, Atlanta, GA
Judy and the late Lawrence Walz, Atlanta, GA
The Cloister, Sea Island, GA
Betsy and Eugene Johnson, Charleston, SC
Jane and Hugh McColl, Charlotte, NC
Ms. Russell Holliday and Mr. Hal Cottingham, Cashiers, NC
Liz and Doug MacIntyre, Charleston, SC
Blickling, England
Colonial Williamsburg Governor's Palace, Williamsburg, VA
Poppy and Rob Clements, Jacksonville, FL
Nancy and Holcombe Green, Cashiers, NC
Chicago Botanical Garden, IL
Cecile and Phil McCaull, Highlands, NC
Thuja Gardens, Asticou Terrace, ME

Wendy and Tom Dowden, Cashiers, NC
Posada Santiago de Aitlan, Lake Aitlan,
    Guatemala
Ruthie and Berryman Edwards, Cashiers, NC
Manningly, England
Sharon Daggett and Andy Tom, Spokane, WA
Compost Pin-Up Men: Charlie Harrison, Marion
    Smith, and Duncan Beard, Atlanta, GA
Philadelphia Flower Show, PA
Asheville Botanical Garden, Asheville, NC
Lonesome Valley, Cashiers, NC
Nancy and Bill Kellman, Charleston, NC
Susan and the late Eric Friberg, Charleston, SC
Norman Askins, Atlanta, GA
Sister Ro and Bill Buchanan, Charleston, SC
Michele and Jimmy Etheredge, Atlanta, GA
Shirley and George Boone, Asheville, NC
Teri and Mose Bond and Fisher and John
    Calame, Highlands, NC
A friend, Atlanta, GA
Marcia and John McCarley, Cashiers, NC
Hippocrates Health Institute,
    West Palm Beach, FL
Bond and Burke Almand, Maryville, TN
Peggy and J. F. Bryan, Cashiers, NC
Gordon and Kinsey Harper, Cashiers, NC
Carol and George Overend, Atlanta, GA
Wisley Gardens, England
Dustin Watson, Cashiers, NC
Ellie and Edward Dobbs, Atlanta, GA
Bridgette and Jerome Dobson, Atlanta, GA
Ann Rawl McCain, Atlanta, GA

High Hampton Inn and Country Club,
    Cashiers, NC
Pat and Carl Hartrampf, Atlanta, GA
Debbie and Robert Fleischer, Waynesville, NC
Teresa and John Gipson, Atlanta, GA
Diane and John Ablon, Charleston, SC
Joan and John Dixon, Mobile, AL
Chattooga Club, Cashiers, NC
Henny and Steve Clay, Atlanta, GA

To the lifelong landscape design aficionados of
any age who read this book and get grounded in
a technological world . . . thank you!

balanced
escapes of REFUGE
and serenity

At a time when life's demands push us to the edge, many are seeking a landscape of refuge and tranquility that is more in harmony with nature. Spaces that restore and offer an escape from our everyday stress have now been proven to enhance healing and longevity. Landscape architect Mary Palmer Dargan offers a new book with a central mission to provide the individual homeowner with a guide to lifelong landscape design.

Building on the principles of Dargan's first book, *Timeless Landscape Design: The Four-Part Master Plan*, she integrated life lessons learned over the course of almost forty years of practice in residential landscape design and a commitment to environments that restore balance, promote well-being and engage lifelong communities. Using both eastern and western design principles, her holistic approach to lifelong landscape design provides a sensitive site development philosophy for existing and new residences. The book explores landscape patterns that inspire health and longevity and provides a how-to guide for creating harmonious outdoor spaces that reduce stress and uplift the body and soul.

Based on years of problem solving with clients and her own personal search for a more sustainable/therapeutic set of design tools, Dargan offers

a much needed method for intergenerational users who seek delight, comfort and a garden that is at ease with its parts. Every chapter is filled with examples and tips honed from her own garden and those designed for others over the years. The information is provided in a way that engages the reader and leaves one eager to get started. *Lifelong Landscape Design* is organized in chapters that correspond to environments identified as essential components of healthy living and include traditional and nontraditional design details presented in an earth-friendly context. Within these landscape patterns are ideas as simple as a chaise lounge to designing a waterfall.

Lifelong Landscape Design synthesizes centuries of principles of design, sustainability and well-being into a new format that is both beautiful to look at and easy to follow with illustrations of more than 100 landscape patterns that provide a blueprint for longevity in the garden. The ideas offered in this inspiring new book will appeal to gardeners at any stage of life.

—Susan L. Hitchcock/Cultural Landscapes Program,
Southeast Regional Office/National Park Service

INTRODUCTION

ROME wasn't built in a day and neither was your GARDEN

THIS FORMAL Scottish garden is a symphony of wildings planted as an understated tapestry.

Lifelong landscape design means thinking about more than your garden. It involves encouraging your community to be a well-rooted environment consisting of friends who share homegrown produce, walk in the neighborhood, recycle, water harvest, compost and are watchful of each other's well-being.

WHY NOT LIVE IN A UTOPIA?

Lifelong communities consist of places that encourage people of all ages to age in place, live as long as they like, and support healthy living by providing connectivity, pedestrian access and transit, neighborhood retail and services, social interaction, a diversity of dwelling types and considerations for existing residents. This is a tall order. Beginning with lifelong landscape design skills and patterns you accumulate through life, building lifelong communities is simply the next step, and the world is a healthier place.

DESIGNING LANDSCAPES TO SPAN A LIFETIME IS A CUMULATIVE PROCESS

Lifelong landscape designs create environments that connect with nature, harmoniously encompass a dwelling and promote healthy living by providing mobility, social interaction and places to sustain the body and soul. Everyone shares hopes and dreams of being vital, healthy members of society. We each need lifelong landscape design training at each stage of life, as young adults and career professionals, families with children or elders who wish and gracefully age in place while staying in their present residence.

NO MATTER HOW SMALL YOUR GARDEN, YOU HAVE TO START SOMEWHERE

Lifelong Landscape Design brings a holistic approach to enhancing health and longevity through the creation of outdoor spaces. In outdoor places, the body and soul is refreshed by connecting with the web of life: the air, water, earth, sun, plant, animal and insect life that interconnect humans and nature. Early in your career, you may garden in a very minimal way with house plants, have flowers in a window box or herbs on a balcony to easily access fresh things to eat. In your forties, if you own a home where you would like to stay for some ten to twenty years or more, it's time to begin the transition to a lifelong landscape. Statistics show that at sixty years of age, 95 percent of homeowners will stay where they currently reside. This is master planning at its best. Love your garden, love yourself.

This book describes the unique branded system I use to design a lifelong landscape for a home. Patterns that interconnect your dwelling with nature and man provide unique and harmonious relationships within a property. This relationship is known as the four-part master plan and opens the door to patterns applicable to any size, style or shape of property in any geographic region. These principles appeared in my earlier book coauthored with Hugh Dargan, *Timeless Landscape Design: The Four-Part Master Plan* (Gibbs Smith, 2007), but are worth repeating here again. Each property has an approach and arrival sequence, the hub of the house, perimeter spaces and destinations with linkages. When a house is at peace with its four parts, it is a better place to live.

This book will transform your property. It is a how-to text and an inspirational guide for individual homeowners. Each chapter is illustrated with project files of real-life landscapes that untangle design problems we've encountered with clients.

LIFELONG LANDSCAPE PATTERNS

Lifelong landscape design is about accumulating a personal language of landscape patterns. No one is born knowing how to garden. We experiment with ways to design outdoor places to meet our changing needs. *Landscape patterns,* the physical elements and arrangements of outdoor spaces, are preferences slowly acquired over time.

People experience several phases in their life-long journey: childhood, single or two-person households, family and elder living. The wonder of nature experienced in childhood gradually gives way to adult living on a balcony, deck or garden. A demanding workplace by day is balanced by outdoor places for stress reduction at home. As single, two-person or family households gradually give way to elder life, the goals for landscape patterns change.

This book explores the principles of lifelong landscape design with rich illustrations of more than 200 landscape patterns. These are as diverse as south-facing exposure for houses, allees, bonsai and pets in the garden. Designers recognize archetypal patterns of how man interacts with the landscape, the way he moves through it, and things he needs to be comfortable, safe and nourished. Explore the multitude of landscape patterns for use, delight and health and you will transform your home environment.

DESIGNING WITH LIFELONG LANDSCAPE PRINCIPLES

Landscape patterns illustrate the nine essential components of healthy living. Lifelong landscape design promotes healthy living for all ages by providing places to sustain the body and soul. Since we are not born knowing how to garden, as we progress through life, we collect landscape patterns that connect man with nature to serve many purposes.

These environments:

* Connect with the web of life
* Encourage social interaction with family and friends
* Offer places for active recreation and play
* Provide passive retreats
* Enhance choices for freedom and access
* Promote evidence-based stress reducers
* Include gardening for health as you tend your wares, your mind and body
* Complement a healthy house with clean air, water and an organized interior plan
* Employ a master plan working seamlessly towards these goals by integrating the four parts inherent of any landscape: the approach and arrival sequence, hub, perimeter and destinations with linkages, plus art elements and design principles and time-honored site-planning techniques.

This may sound like a tall order but, like any complex project, once broken into components, it is easy to see the proverbial forest for the trees.

IT IS TIME TO GET STARTED

Lifelong landscape design offers your personal residence a tune-up, a way to harmonize its parts. Provide a healthy environment and activities for intergenerational users in your family. Reconnect with the web of life and heal the world one garden at a time while creating unique outdoor areas to sustain body and soul.

Inspiration is found perched; on top of a mountain, Ushuata connects earth and man. Whatever happens here rains down upon the valley below and the owners are careful to control water runoff.

CHAPTER 1

The Web of Life

The *web of life* is the interrelationship of man and nature, whereby a balance is achieved through judiciously shared resources. Small ponds, rivulets, and butterfly, rain or wild gardens are landscape types that invite nature to be appreciated at close range. This is the first of the nine principles of lifelong landscape design and provides many archetypal landscape patterns.

Simply being in nature offers positive health benefits. Evidence-based landscape design reveals that interaction with nature reduces stress. Your body and mind relax when you enjoy a woodland walk or quietly read in the shade, and this reduces your cortisol level, a known physiological stressor.

Rest Lightly on the Land

The interface between soft and hardscape is cleverly integrated by using crab orchard stones set into grass in a random ashlar pattern in the O'Leary garden in Atlanta, Georgia, and helps Mother Nature by soaking up excess water from rain.

Outdoor rooms, terraces, decks and arbors are environments that encourage connection with the web of life by providing a flat space for entertaining or relaxation. In a lifelong landscape, the approach and arrival sequence, the hub, perimeter and destinations of the house set the stage for connection with nature. The seamless integration of these four parts becomes your home's own personal web of life. Lifestyle needs, like a convenient compost center or movement from the car, can *rest lightly on the land* when constructed of sustainable materials.

Resting lightly on the land is a thoughtful design process. Holistic, in that ecological and functional properties of your home grounds are integrated like a fine engine; this process determines how the parts of your landscape system behaves. By employing both eastern and western site-planning principles, holistic landscape design provides a sensitive site development philosophy for existing and new residences. Sustainability principles, such as *leave nature alone, restore nature's balance, sculpt your niche thoughtfully, use flexible building materials, consider origins of supplies, pave less, harvest and conserve water, let nature rest*, and *keep up the good work*, are foundations for holistic and lifelong landscape design.

DEVELOPING A PHILOSOPHY

The web of life is intricate and complex. Mother Nature evolved a set of holistic interconnections that existed on this planet long before man evolved as hunter-gatherer. I call it the *web of life* to punctuate how nature relates to man in a fragile, tangible and symbiotic way. The ecological niche occupied by man evolved slowly over thousands of sleepy generations, then catapulted into the computer age in one frenetic, generational burst.

Centuries of man's industrial relationship with the land resulted in much heavy-handed development practices. Habitat destruction and degradation of the air, water and soil lead the pack of man's intrusions. Over-exploitation of food, pets, introduced species, pollution and disease resulted as man profited from the environment without moderation. Without a crystal ball to divine future repercussions, climate change is now recognized as a serious threat. The world's biodiversity is declining at an unprecedented rate, according to the IUCN Red List, the global watchdog on endangered species. Current extinction rates are at least 100 to 1,000 times higher than natural rates found in the fossil record. A startling decline of 73 percent occurs in primates.

You can help the world recover, one garden at a time, by beginning with your plot of ground. A holistic landscape philosophy is worth pursuing to produce the most sensitive site development on your property.

Leave nature in peace. This simple woodland stream in Joyce Kilmer Forest is doing far more to perpetuate its precious niche on the planet than any re-created landscape.

Six Tenets of Sustainable Landscape DESIGN

The web of life is intricate and complex. By keeping the tenets of sustainability at the forefront of design, you are one step further toward consciously helping Mother Nature.

Sustainability techniques are *do no harm, restore nature's balance, sculpt your niche thoughtfully, use flexible building materials, consider origins of supplies, pave less, harvest and conserve water, let nature rest, and keep up the good work.* These tenets are all underlying foundations for holistic, lifelong landscape design.

TENET #1: LEAVE NATURE ALONE
It is often more difficult to keep a property healthy than to create a healthy new place.

Trees are valuable, fragile and often taken for granted. For instance, mature trees are far more fragile than you might imagine. Trees in construction zones often slowly regress, drop branches and eventually die over a period of four or five years. This loss of vitality is completely avoidable and seldom considered. Compaction from construction equipment

crossing over soft ground above roots compresses the earth, squeezing out the interstitial spaces that provide for respiration between root, water and oxygen. A cushion of six inches of chopped mulch, perhaps from site clearing, will mitigate this situation.

Defining corridors for traffic, if even just for light-duty cars and workers' trucks, is highly effective. Using chain-linked fence or silt protection fence backed with wire to outline the drive and parking areas is a simple technique that will save lives of trees.

Mountaintops and beachfronts are to be treated with great respect. They are fragile. With soils created by eons of gentle wind and water action, the ecosystems that sprung up support more interconnected, biodynamic activities than you can imagine.

TENANT #2 : RESTORE THE BALANCE OF NATURE
So many ways exist to injure a site; the cost to ameliorate is slow and staggering.

Excavated chasms and banks in the mountains

PROJECT FILE
A Blank Canvas

FROM HURRICANE and floods to tornadoes and white fly infestations, the South has seen plenty of extreme activity in the past few years. Friends George and Anne Peagler of Americas, Georgia, sent us photos of their devastated home, wrecked by an EF3 tornado on March 1, 2007. A blank canvas was left in the wake of the disaster in a hitherto mature setting. Having lost their roof and a car as well, they bravely seized upon the opportunity to create a southern stroll garden. Included in the master plan was the vision of a lake. Within three years, magnolias, crepe myrtles, camellias, azaleas and a host of favorite shrubs were employed to screen the house from the road as well as to create a winding set of paths. Today it is a utopia with shady benches and leisurely walkways.

A steep slope conducts water with blinding speed in a rainfall. When denuded of trees, precious topsoil is swept off the hillside and into surrounding streams, suffocating insects upon which trout feed.

on highway rights of ways certainly illustrate the power of man over nature. The sheer height of a cut bank, be it clay or stone, is an unnatural visage. Erosion, the drift of clay and soil fines from one spot to another, can cause enormous environmental impact.

The siltation of streams literally smothers the invertebrates that live in the waters. A fine covering of dust-like silt on gravel in a creek bed is enough to keep insect eggs from maturing and therefore providing larvae for fish to eat. There goes the native trout population. When the silt becomes really deep in natural ponds, it makes the water shallower and warmer. This again is detrimental to trout, since they cannot reproduce in warm water when the temperature gets as little as three degrees above its average temperature. The trout are but one of many steps in the food chain; other animals depend on trout to eat for survival.

Topsoil, when stripped from a site, is often saved aside. It is virtually impossible to rebuild woodland, even with preserved topsoil and the best biodiversity science can muster. In a garden, a healthy soil layer can be created, similar to natural duff, by harvesting every sack of leaves you can find. Scour your neighborhood in the fall and investigate the leaf sacks beside the road and harvest heavier ones with mower-mulched leaves. Spread these found treasures on top of your barren earth at a depth of three to four inches and let sit all winter. It sounds labor intensive, but it will degrade into some nice stuff by spring. Soil fertility and structure is a lengthy topic and many references are available online, via magazines such as *Organic Gardening* and in bookstores.

Another way to rebuild a damaged ecosystem is to plant baby trees. Trees Atlanta and other urban forestry programs provide trees at a good price for community improvement. You can also become your own local Johnny Appleseed, like John McCarley of Cashiers, who grows baby spruce from seed, backpacks them to mountainsides and transplants with a sip of water from his canteen. They magically take hold. With the decline in the native hemlock due to wholly adelgid, his actions will preserve both habitat and reduce erosion for future decades.

LEFT: Sustainable building materials are used to absorb water, such as in this drive, where grass is used as a layby for occasional parking.

BELOW: The stepping-stones are set into grass to allow water to percolate into the ground and recharge the ground water, and large river gravel for a driveway takes the place of a less porous surface.

TENET #3: SCULPT YOUR NICHE USING SUSTAINABLE BUILDING MATERIALS

Sustainable landscape construction is about thoughtful choices in building materials.

Are you considering a new or improved parking area? "Going green" can be as simple as installing a natural brown gravel instead of asphalt. Asphalt is a black, bituminous product that takes a lot of oil to produce. Although it is composed of natural products, it has a high carbon footprint. A little research will provide a wealth of options.

Concrete now comes in pervious paving choices that capture ground water and allow it to seep into the ground, thus reducing storm-water runoff. Carefully controlled amounts of water and cement-forming materials are used to create a paste that forms a thick coating around aggregate particles. A pervious concrete mixture contains little or no sand, creating a substantial void content and is primarily used in pavement.

Packed gravel of local origin is one of my favorites. Natural colors of buff and gray, enhanced by river action on rocky pebbles, creates a beautiful natural finish. A two-inch layer of larger stone on top of crushed gravel, running base is preferred. Most slopes more than 12 percent will require a more stable surfacing such as cobbles or pavers to reduce erosion.

BELOW: This simple pond is 8 x 14 feet and collects water runoff into the woodland, thereby providing a place for frogs to breed.

RIGHT: At the Asheville Arboretum in Asheville, North Carolina, a display of sustainable practices shows water-harvesting techniques such as rain barrels and cisterns, plus composting techniques such as bullet composers. These principles are essential kit for lifelong landscapes.

TENET #4: HARVEST AND CONSERVE WATER

Harvesting water for home garden consumption is a stewardship act.

To solve water needs, it is best to look at your property as a whole, a mini "watershed" waiting to be harvested. Your roof, driveway and garden areas compose a drainage system. Best practice dictates to enlist a storm-water expert to help size a cistern or multiple tanks, determine where to place them, and to know exactly how much water your property needs. Of course, a rain garden can be designed in low areas that naturally receive water. Rain barrels are useful on a gutter-by-gutter basis, so an overflow area is necessary. Overall, underground tanks are the best storage system, and investment in an expert to install a proper overflow, pump and irrigation system is money well spent.

Of course, harvesting and conserving water revolves around more than cisterns and temporary storage systems. Understanding your environment and the native and introduced plants that are compatible with your site is paramount. Horticultural prowess, the use of permeable surfaces and thoughtful planning for functional space are design considerations. Sharpen your pencil and plan ahead!

Timberline in Cashiers, North Carolina, enhances evening experiences with low-voltage lights to encourage safe, pleasant garden use at night. A variety of fixtures illuminate where light is needed. These lights use little energy, and timers operate on a regular basis for a limited amount of hours to lessen impact on wildlife. The Outdoor Lights, a site-sensitive lighting company, provided coordination and installation.

TENET #5: LET NATURE REST

Let there be a minimum of light, mostly low and small.

Nightlights. Garden visits along dimly lit paths. The garump of a frog. Listening with a beverage in hand. Laughter. The romantic wonder of nature at night. These are a few of my favorite things. Gardens at night are very special. However, the wonder of nightscapes can be ruined by harsh headlights, unsafe changes in grade such as terraced steps, or trails that leave too much to the imagination.

Design for nighttime use is as simple and creative as your fixtures and their placement. Any fixture, be it bottle light, Amish hammered tin, a Mexican star light or a coal lantern, once wired and connected to an electrical source, can be a quiet, atmospheric light source. Use the lowest-wattage bulb you can, such as a 9-volt refrigerator battery or chandelier light. Employ an automatic timer that comes on at dusk (change it seasonally) and goes off at 11 p.m. Birds like this.

TENET #6 : KEEP UP THE GOOD WORK

The devil is in the details and maintenance is next to godliness.

Taking good care of your property is a steward-ship principle. Healthy lifelong landscapes have a natural life cycle of mowing and chopping or har-vesting leaves, composting, mulching and spread-ing, weeding, and more mulching and spreading.

I look at my garden clippings, rakings, lawn trash and deadheads as compost. This is a harvest that ebbs and tides in the garden. Right now, it

is a very heavy early summer harvest. We have clumps of clippings in large piles that will quickly decompose but need management.

Compost management is but a small part of your maintenance plan. Understanding organic pest control, fertilization, soil chemistry, microbes and drainage mitigation is a lifelong landscape pursuit. It is a process of using a calendar and intu-ition to assess the seasonal needs of the property, disciplined nurturing of your garden and knowl-edge, and conscious study of ways to improve the health of your environment.

Ushuata:
Where the Earth Ends and Dreams Begin

USHUATA IS a Native American Cherokee term for "Where earth ends and dreams begin" and describes a home site with beauty and brains. As a superior example of sustainable landscape practices, Ushuata addresses more than thirty-five documented points of sustainable practices and their performance over time. The landscape artistry is informed by the unique genius loci on top of a mountain.

The owners' brief was to restore the damaged site's ecosystem, reduce resource consumption and integrate the land-scape design with the emerging architecture to produce a home environ-ment that honors its set-ting. The house complex is clad in tulip-poplar bark, a local byproduct of the logging industry, and is perched above a dynamic view punctuated by steep granite gneiss bluffs.

Ushuata is a personal botanical garden, to be enjoyed in all seasons, and witnesses the diversity of native and introduced plantings adaptable to

With architecture by the architectural firm of Meyer, Greeson, Paullin and Benson of Charlotte, North Carolina, Ushuata features vernacular, sustainable materials and a traditional housing form reminiscent of an early farmhouse.

severe climatic change. The design encompassed the entire property.

The Rain Garden at the "big view" overlook absorbs and disperses water during major storms to reduce siltation and erosion to the mountainside below Ushuata. We selected locally available plants to create a botanical garden for zone 5. It includes a cutting and butterfly garden, a stroll garden, native plants in mossy woodland and conifer proving ground on terraces. A herb and provisions garden for family use is adjacent the kitchen entrance.

The property is el 4,410 feet and overlooks a picturesque lake approximately three-quarters mile distant. Rainfall (87.75 inches yearly) can be thirty-six inches in a summer month. Alternately, it can be as dry as a bone. The very thin, granite dust soils have little fertility.

The owners, to provide water for irrigation, previously constructed an existing 28,000-gallon cistern on the site. Lighting and winds are severe.

Newly built, broad plateaus provide both intimacy and offer 280-degree views to encompass surrounding mountains. To reduce the feeling of "falling off a cliff," five stone terraces featuring native stone and rustic steps provide transitional spaces between

upper garden and parking court. Despite the twenty-two-foot drop in elevation, the gardens are cozy, and the woodland provides shelter for botanical specimens and native plants. Natives are encouraged to self-seed.

The arrival sequence features a permeable, native river gravel drive bordered by nuggets of local crab orchard stone. The parking court and front entry is paved with gravel and large slabs.

Native plantings are along the drive.

The overlook terrace is retained by a twenty-foot-tall perimeter boulder wall. This large plateau supports a 37,500-gallon capacity of water harvested from four tanks with filters. It provides grassy lawns for children to play and is rimmed with rustic, black locust splitrail fencing and four tiers of espaliered apple branches as a living screen.

The broad plateaus at Ushuata conceal large cisterns that provide 37,500 gallons of water harvested from the property to provide fire protection and irrigation. John Warren of Natural Landscapes in Cashiers, North Carolina, installed the entire project designed by Dargan Landscape Architects.

Rain Gardens at Ushuata collect water prior to discharge and encourage a gentle seeping of overflow onto the fragile mountain surrounding the property. The stone edging is lowered to grass level to allow water to cross into the bed and pond.

Landscape Patterns for Sustainable ACTIVITIES

Landscape patterns provide a candy box of ideas for your garden. Chosen to connect you with the web of life, they also illustrate activities you can undertake to connect with the web, such as raising bees, composting or propagating goldfish.

This library of landscape patterns features a graphic icon, photograph or detail such as a bench niche or allee. Alphabetized for easy reference, this system provides a lexicon of inspirational ideas to help visualize areas in your landscape. Only a sampling is offered in this book. The full library is located at www.dargan.com/landscapeyourlife.

Keep in mind that many of these ideas and images easily work for other chapters. We chose these as shortcuts to accessing the web of life and are valuable additions to your life-long master plan.

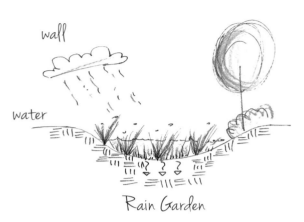

wall

water

Rain Garden

Lifelong
Landscape
Patterns and
PLACES

RAIN GARDEN

Rain gardens are planted depressions or swales in the earth that reduce storm-water runoff by capturing and filtering water from impervious surfaces like roofs, driveways and parking lots. Because of this ability to capture and slow down water, rain gardens improve water quality in nearby water bodies.

While rain gardens are a highly functional way to help protect water quality, they are also gardens and should be an attractive part of your yard and neighborhood.

❉ When choosing native plants for the garden, it is important to consider the height of each plant, bloom time and color, and its overall texture. Use plants that bloom at different times to create a long flowering season. Mix heights, shapes and textures to give the garden depth and dimension.

* When laying out plants, randomly clump individual species in groups of three to seven plants to provide a bolder statement of color. Make sure to repeat these individual groupings to create repetition and cohesion in a planting.
* Try incorporating a diverse mixture of sedges, rushes and grasses with your flowering species (forbs). In natural areas, a diversity of plant types not only adds beauty but also creates a thick underground root matrix that keeps the entire plant community in balance. In fact, 80 percent of the plant mass in native plant communities is underground.

Planting the Rain Garden

Select plants that have a well-established root system. Usually one- or two-year-old plants will have root systems that are beginning to circle or get matted. (Note: Use only nursery-propagated plants; do not collect plants from the wild.)

Dig each hole twice as wide as the plant plug and deep enough to keep the crown of the young plant level with the existing grade (just as it was growing in the cell pack or container). Make sure the crown is level and then fill the hole and firmly tamp around the roots to avoid air pockets.

Apply double-shredded mulch evenly over the bed approximately two inches thick, but avoid burying the crowns of the new transplants. Mulching is usually not necessary after the second growing season unless the "mulched look" is desired.

As a general rule, plants need one inch of water per week. Water immediately after planting and continue to water twice a week until the plugs are established. You should not have to water your rain garden once the plants are established.

RILLS, RIVULETS AND STREAMS

A rill is a man-made, narrow rivulet of water that leads the eye along its curving or straight path. Historically, rills are a device used since the early geometric period to convey drama and mystery. They are unnatural but beautiful to behold. Stone bordered and filled with water-loving plants, the rill played an organizational role in Arts and Crafts gardens, separating the badminton court, for instance, from the tea party. I long for a rill but must settle for a rivulet instead.

Depending on the run of the rill, rivulet or stream, generally a medium-sized pump will do if the terrain is flat. Like all bodies of water, your rill or rivulet must be contained. In Morocco, clay tiles form a channel of water; in Portugal, the rill is lined with tiles. In America, a plastic black liner set as a small swale will accomplish the look and feel of a rill. Fish are generally not included—unless they escape from your pond! Rills may be filled by hand or an automatic system, and like all water features, may be pumped and recycled.

Just large enough for a few goldfish, this pond at the bottom of the long slope at Timberline is planted with horsetails and ferns to mimic a natural water body, and it's surrounded with large boulders so children can get close to the water.

Small Pond

SMALL POND

Hugh and I claimed possession of an unloved patch of land in the middle of our driveway and created our first basin, fed it ten goldfish and dubbed it "Anniversary Pond." As simple as could be, this unfiltered pond, filled by a water hose and rain water, was dug as large as possible to accommodate a liner 16 x 16 feet square. We cut and shaped the liner to curve slightly into the bend of the drive, dug the

hole, rolled back the liner edges to hold water and stuck river rocks around the perimeter. An aquarium pump added a modicum of movement through the broken arm of my great uncle's crumbling cupid.

Our pond is 100 percent homemade, and for two landscape architects to proudly present this unsophisticated pond to friends ten years ago was laughable. The goldfish flourished and reproduced by the hundreds. Pondweeds are now

happy; water lilies took hold and multiplied.

We think the best-looking ponds mimic nature. River rocks line the bottom, and sides should be sized anywhere from five to eight feet wide. Make the pond no more than three feet deep with shelves. Fill the pond by hose or automatic system. We extended an irrigation pipe to add water every third day in the dry season. A ground fault switch provides electricity and the small fountain pump is easily changed.

Now the fun part, the fish! Provide stone shelves for fish to hide from raccoons and herons. Don't feed your fish or they will, Pavlov-like, rise to the surface whenever shadows cross and get scooped up by varmints. Let them feed off the plantings. We love basic golden orfes, goldfish and shubunkins. We clean and compost large debris from the pond once a year; thus, the pond is a maintenance dream.

LEFT: At Heale House, one of our favorite English gardens, the arched pergola of apples provides a shady walk.

FACING: A parking lot fit for a party! A sizzling display of cohosh punctuates the drive at Debbie and Fleischer's home in Balsam Mountain Preserve in Waynesville, North Carolina.

TRELLISED WALK OR PERGOLA

A pleasant, transitional space that offers enclosure on a leisurely walk, the English referred to these structures as pergolas. Used for perambulations in the shade, they help shape outdoor spaces and emphasize a walk. A typical size is five feet wide and ten feet long. Visit Dumbarton Oaks in Washington, D.C., or Hampton Court Palace outside London to see the perfect pergola based on historical models with groin vaults and barrel arches, featured in *Timeless Landscape Design.*

WILD AND WOODLAND GARDENS

Wild and woodland gardens may consist of native plants or be a mix of ornamental and natural plantings such as grasses, mosses, ground covers, large and small shrubs, and evergreen and deciduous trees. Plantings are installed as if they occurred naturally without formal edges or bedding. Through this process, the natural balance is enhanced, not threatened.

These gardens tend to be self-regulated. This balance, achieved in some of the oldest English gardens, today looks entirely like a natural

setting. A formula for creating a new woodland walk is to begin with encouraging natural leaf litter to enrich the soil. Cut timber allowed to decompose naturally will eventually provide fine topsoil. Collect leaf bags from the side of the road in the fall and spread them around the new garden. Weeds may join the leaves, but these are easily roughed out.

Choosing plants depends on the amount and diversity of trees. Woodland walks are shaded environments. In a natural setting, there are low-growing ephemerals, such as trillium,

that emerge only in the spring when trees are deciduous. A second tier of taller plants consists of ferns and evergreen plants such as hellebores. Emerging from this ground-cover mix are the small and large evergreen shrubs such as native azaleas, which form natural-looking patches. Depending on the amount of high dappled shade, a wide variety of small trees will flourish and provide perches and nesting sites for birds. When designing woodland, think about providing habitat for birds to rest, so they will nest, and feed so they will breed.

FACING: A mossy walk invites a ramble at Ushuata. River rocks line the path and the bark chip covering provides a pleasant and sustainable surface.

RIGHT: Gerard McCann keeps bees in the urban midtown area of Atlanta. Sheltered by shady trees and complemented by a chicken coup nearby, Gerard provides homes for several hives as a hobby. He serves the community by moving unwanted colonies from public places and relocating them to a new home.

Lifelong
Landscape
ACTIVITIES

BENEFICIAL INSECTS: BEES

What is the first thing that comes to mind when you think of bees? Honey or flowers? What about tomatoes, onions, carrots, and hundreds of other fruits and vegetables—and livestock? No human activity can ever replace the work of bees yet their work is largely taken for granted. Bees pollinate about one-sixth of the world's flowering plant species and approximately 400 agricultural plants. A 2000 Cornell University study concluded that bees contribute more than $14.6 billion to U.S. agriculture through pollination. The U.S. Department of Agriculture estimates that about one-third of what we eat is pollinated by insects, and honeybees are responsible for 80 percent of that pollination. Plants that are poorly pollinated are oftentimes lower yielding, misshapen and lower quality—consequences that affect the price and availability of food.

Having bees in your home garden will not only contribute to your personal plant species collection but will also benefit the flowers, fruits and vegetables of surrounding areas—sometimes miles away. Pollen is one of the purest natural foods. It consists of 35 percent protein and 10 percent sugars, as well as carbohydrates, enzymes, minerals and multiple vitamins. Eating a small amount of pollen every day, from local honey sources, will help reduce symptoms of pollen-related allergies. Bees are the only insect that produces food eaten by humans and honey is the only food that includes all of the substances necessary to sustain life.

COMPOST

Composting is not only an easy way to significantly reduce personal waste, but it is also a wonderful and natural way for organic waste to be processed. Nutrient-rich compost is great for gardening, tree pits and even indoor plants. And unlike traditional recycling where you send your glass/plastic/cardboard to a recycling plant, with composting you can actually see every step of the natural recycling process. Composting has a huge effect on lowering waste reduction impact. In fact, the U.S. EPA estimates that each American throws away an average of 1.3 pounds of food scraps daily; the combination of this waste, along with yard trimmings, contributes to 24 percent of our nation's solid waste stream.

A composting area is functionally the heart of your landscape but not very attractive placed in the middle of your garden. Often shielded behind a fence, the assorted compost bins, tumblers, tools and tea makers of a fully expressed compost center take up a good bit of space. You never stop composting. There is a path from the house with kitchen green matter and select paper goods, a path from the

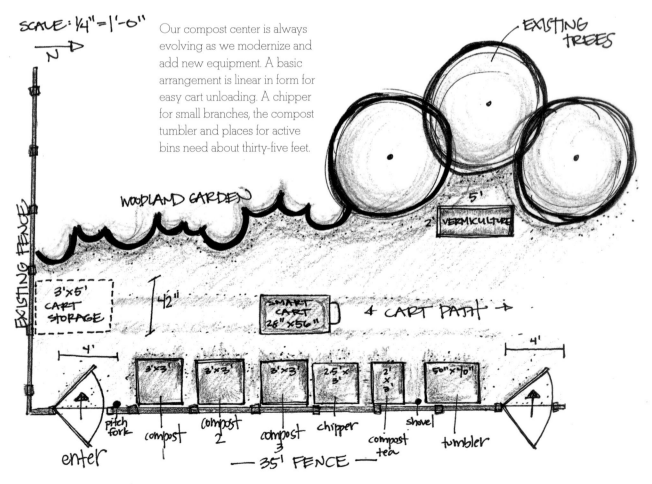

SCALE: 1/4" = 1'-0"
N↑

Our compost center is always evolving as we modernize and add new equipment. A basic arrangement is linear in form for easy cart unloading. A chipper for small branches, the compost tumbler and places for active bins need about thirty-five feet.

EXISTING TREES

WOODLAND GARDEN

EXISTING FENCE

5'

2' VERMICULTURE

3'x5' CART STORAGE

42"

SMART CART 28"x56"

4 CART PATH →

4'

4'

3'x3'

2'x3'

3'x3'

2.5'x 3'

2' x 3'

50"x 70"

enter

pitch fork

compost

compost 2

compost 3

chipper

compost tea

shovel

tumbler

— 35' FENCE —

garden with clippings and weeds, and there is access from the toolshed for pitchforks and wheelbarrows.

At Highcote, we put our compost center behind the fence that encloses the kitchen garden. Here we have a little shed roof approximately eight feet long and four feet deep where clippers and the chipper are kept out of the elements. Along the backside of the fence, we place wheelbarrows and rakes, large shovels and bulky objects such as fertilizer bins. The compost tumbler is accessed where it can be loaded or unloaded using the large garden cart, and a four-foot path links it all together.

Compost tea is made from steeping compost in water and extracting the juice, or tea. This tea may be used as a foliar spray or a soil drench. We use comfrey and soak it in plastic trash cans, pumping or pouring it onto the garden plants after about three weeks of fermenting. It has a pretty high smell, so we are careful to plan garden visits before spraying.

Why go through all the effort of making tea instead of using "regular" compost? Compost tea extends the benefits of its original counterpart. When sprayed directly on the leaves, it helps control foliar diseases as well as increases the amount of nutrients available to the plant. It also speeds the breakdown of toxins.

Compost is gold and takes some elbow grease. You need space to be creative! Our six-foot fence separates the kitchen garden from the compost center and does double duty as a tool storage area.

VERMICULTURE

Vermiculture is a process that uses worms to decompose organic waste. Vermicomposting is different than other compost systems because it can be done inside—making it more accessible to the average family. A single person using a small worm bin can produce about thirty pounds of compost in four months! The Len Foote Hike Inn, a LEED gold medal backcountry lodge in Amicalola, Georgia, utilizes vermiculture for all its dining refuse in four 8 x 4-foot beds located in an unheated shed. Vermiculture boxes are not complicated nor is the process.

How can you get started? There are many vermiculture kits available today. Two popular kits are the Worm Factory and the UrBin Grower.

The Worm Factory, made by Cascade Sales, Inc., features an easy-to-use, odorless operation; it is compact, making it easy for indoor or outdoor use; it is expandable; and it is made in the USA with recycled materials. The Worm Factory is virtually odorless when used correctly, and the multi-tray system separates the worms from the compost for you—no more time spent turning piles or removing worms by hand! How does the Worm Factory work?

Start with the bottom tray and add a handful of organic waste and worms. The worms will immediately begin to process the food. Once the bottom tray is filled, stack another tray on top of it—gradually, the worms will work their way up to the newest food and leave nutrient waste below.

The UrBin Grower is also sold by Cascade Sales, Inc., and serves as a counterpart to the Worm Factory. Not unlike the Worm Factory, the UrBin Grower is perfect for urban families and comes in portable multipurpose containers. Using the Square Foot Gardening method,

natural soil amendments, and a self-watering reservoir, the UrBin Grower can provide an abundance of organic vegetables. In order to continue and promote good health, fourteen essential and trace nutrients are included with the grower—this allows you to control the quality of food that you and your family consume. Because of chemical fertilizers and groundwater pollution, trace minerals are depleted from almost all agricultural land. These trace minerals are extremely beneficial to plants, animals, and humans, and are transferred through vegetables grown in rich soils.

The owners of this elegant
Buckhead home in Atlanta
waited seven years for the
wisteria to bloom and now
hold a luncheon to honor
it each year!

CHAPTER 2

Social Places

Structuring your home environment for outdoor use is a wish list that never seems to end! Do you long for venues, recreation and entertainment areas to accommodate activities outside the house? Whether dining al fresco on a terrace for intimate dining or watching small children at play close at hand, outdoor-use areas provide health and pleasure. At any stage of life, changing priorities can nudge outdoor spaces to morph into better ways to entertain, garden and enjoy wildlife. In a world of dwindling living space, the pressure is on to design these places to peacefully coexist in the *perimeter* of the house— approximately seventy to a hundred feet from the house. The perimeter is a type of pattern language, an integral part of mankind's home landscape from time immemorial.

Perimeter spaces are often used for entertainment and activity. Packing complementary uses into one area is known as multipurpose space. A good example is a dining terrace complete with a spa adjacent to vegetables planted in pots that has a carefully designed footprint that takes advantage of environment and spatial opportunity.

Each part of your four-part master plan—*the approach and arrival sequence, hub, perimeter and linkages to destinations*—has a landscape pattern, or use areas with unique dimensions and spatial layout. This graphic language consists of typical movement and arrangement of features by man in space.

The Clements family in Jacksonville, Florida, enjoys casual grilling on the porch and gathering around the pool. The lawn easily tents for a large party convenient to pool house and catering. Richard Skinner, architect, designed the addition and pool house.

Encourage Social Interaction with Family and Friends: DINING AND GROUP ACTIVITIES

Social gatherings at any stage of life are healthy. Proximity to others for conversation encourages healthy mental and physical development. Social outdoor environments include places for setting up furniture, such as pavilions, loggias, terraces, decks and lawns. A grill, outdoor kitchen and fireplace extend the seasonal use of a social outdoor area. A bench niche, especially when placed under a refuge tree, is convenient for a conversation between grandparent and child, or two lovers.

Children benefit from outdoor dining areas where they can learn reacting to random acts of nature. They gain expertise in adapting to insects, sun and wind in a social environment early in life and carry outdoor dining skills into adulthood. Hugh and I learned as young adults in Charleston, South Carolina, where historic houses are the size of a postage stamp, that outdoor dining takes the pressure off a small house to perform for a larger group. Families utilize outdoor dining for casual multigenerational events; an additional food station or bar sets up well on a terrace and enhances traffic flow through the house. Elders enjoy outdoor dining for the sheer ability to access the outdoors freely and to share it with others.

Careful space planning is indicated in social environments. A table for two or four families takes a certain amount of space due to the constraints of the human form.

Lifelong Landscape Patterns
AND PLACES

The following outdoor areas encourage and promote social interaction in numerous settings.

ARBOR

This half-roof, half-sky place is delightfully romantic. Arbors also provide shade and transitional overhead enclosure as one steps from house to terrace or garden.

LEFT: How large should an arbor be and where should it go? The best rule of thumb is to treat it like an outdoor room. Plan your furniture and space and then roof the area. We often use an 8 x 12-foot arbor and deck combination. Frankie Hargrove Interiors of Cashiers, North Carolina, provided the furniture fabric.

BELOW: Nestled into a cozy border adjacent to the great lawn, this bench is great for a quiet conversation while watching butterflies in the cutting garden at Ron Calabrese and Cristine Cozzins' Atlanta home.

BENCH NICHE

A place to sit is a rare commodity. Somehow, a bench or chair gets left out of the gardens because of lack of understanding concerning its placement. Place benches in a semiprivate space or in a nook with views outward. Benches work best if surrounded by soft and lush plant materials full of color and fragrance.

Formula for a Great Deck

GENERALLY OF wood, iroko or teak, and structurally connected to a house and projected above the ground, a deck as small as 8 x 8 feet or as large as a ballroom floor can be designed. Decks can be limited to balconies or part of an outdoor room with steps to reach terra firma. Front porches can also be built like a deck for inexpensive access to the door landing.

Inspiration: At Phantom Forest in Knysna on the Garden Route of South Africa, an eco-lodge had a series of extended decks high above trees filled with monkeys. The decks were spacious enough to serve eighteen guests and have a warming fire in the middle.

Best Looking: The best look is achieved by using teak or iroko flooring in a herringbone pattern with a gossamer, twisted metal cable around the perimeter.

Size: The best deck size for small families is 18 x 20 feet with a grill. For larger groups, consider making a deck two tiered. Decks are much like rooms; once their proportions are stretched, they feel awkward.

Utilities: Use electrical for ambient lighting and add gas for a grill and water if a sink is included in the design.

LEFT: A tiny birdhouse of a cottage is summer home to Nashville friends, architect Martin Shofner and Corabel. Nestled in the trees, this deck aerie provides the perfect place to perch and ponder the adjacent waterfall.

FACING: This deck is conveniently located near the kitchen and dining area designed by Brevard architect Al Platt. Surrounded by white tardiva and limelight hydrangeas, the deck appears to float in a cloud.

LEFT: The Baxter arbor offers shaded seating nested at the end of an allee of Chinese sumac in Las Vegas.

FURNITURE

Every functional outdoor space needs furniture. It allows people to sit and enjoy the beauty around them and encourages both social interaction and interaction with the great outdoors. Whether the look is modern or mountain, furniture is a great way to accessorize your garden, deck or terrace.

GRILLS

A grill is a must-have for any outdoor-oriented family or individual. It creates social spaces and areas for interaction. Whether you have a small charcoal grill or a large gas grill built into an outdoor kitchen, it is sure to be enjoyed by all.

FIREPLACES

An outdoor fireplace acts as a great hub or focal point. People will naturally be drawn to

its beauty and warmth, no matter the size.
Whether it is made of brick or stone, a fireplace
is always a beautiful and functional addition to
your outdoor space.

LOGGIA

Commonly seen in Italian architecture, loggias are
corridors at ground level (or higher) that are connected to the façade of a building. They are open
on the other side, which allows for air circulation.

BELOW: When Margaret Wills called to say she needed a flat place to expand, this lovely shape came to mind immediately. It's like a very pretty rug when viewed from the screen porch above and it opens conveniently from the house for parties.

LOWER: My favorite fire pit belongs to Bill and Susan Young high above Lake Glenville, near Cashiers, North Carolina. Their three-foot-diameter pit provides just enough heat for a romantic tête-à-tête outside to watch the sunset.

FIRE PIT

Do you long for a roasted marshmallow? A fire pit may be for you. Not all fire pits are created equal; some are deep in the ground and fired by propane, others are wood fired. Each needs a drain in the bottom for rainy day excess. Fire platforms are also fun and feature a raised seating area that is easy to light and remove but offers little wind resistance.

Until we built the Pavilion of Pleasant Sounds, our property was incomplete. We also call it the outdoor kitchen, and nothing is more pleasing than to fire up the pizza oven and cook a bruschetta with tomatoes from our kitchen garden. The pavilion sits next to a series of ponds where frogs sing and fish swim.

TAPIS VERT

A tapis vert is an unbroken expanse of lawn and is used as a major element in the landscape.

RETREAT/PAVILION

Retreats and pavilions are the quintessential destination. Everything from a deep six-foot arbor with a four-foot bench to an outdoor kitchen counts as a retreat. A retreat is out of visual connection with other parts of the property. It is private. It offers intimacy, possibly a view and is often associated with entertainment and dining. The outdoor kitchen is a popular retreat and includes extended surfaces for cooking and many places for seating. Access to a pavilion is essential. Wide paths that accommodate a golf cart or large-wheeled cart improve the functional aspects of pavilion service for parties.

The Perfect Outdoor Room

ANOTHER COURTYARD, owned by Mary and Rick Inman, required some rehabilitation. Working with existing walls and adding a segment to finish the enclosure created the perfect courtyard space. Featuring a fountain, grill and table for six to dine, it works as a sun pocket in the winter for family gatherings.

Outdoor rooms connected to common rooms in the house are enclosed, which gives the feeling of a room, even though it is open to the sky. Columns or trees can help define the corners of a space. A partial "roof" can be created with a trellis or a sliding canvas roof. "Walls" can be constructed of fences, screens or hedges. Outdoor rooms as living spaces can be as small as 8 x 8 feet for two people or 18 x 21 feet, such as a large tent.

Outdoor rooms have multiple components:

Hedges: A wall composed of plants; e.g., boxwood, Japanese holly, yew, forsythia, abelia or azalea.

Green Walls: Use small-leafed vines/climbing plants; e.g., cotoneaster, Virginia creeper, creeping fig, bougainvillea, clematis, English ivy, grape, jasmine, trumpet vine or wisteria. Use your imagination to create enclosure and privacy.

RURAL RETREAT

Hidden coves and hollows have a spirit, or "genius loci," that brings legends and folklore alive in this part of east Tennessee. This spirit was consulted and tapped for inspiration while designing the site plan for Toad Hall. The brief was to include a log residence, historic log structures, a passageway barn, a stone bank barn, writer's cottage and potting shed.

The whole site is a garden with native herbs, shrubs, herbaceous orchids and trees pathside around the lake and formalized closer to the house with antique roses in a period kitchen garden. Natural materials, such as rustic locust posts as lamp standards, tumbled cobblestone edging and large weathered stepping-stones placed in grass, immediately give the log home a settled feeling.

Toad Hall is reached after a long pastoral drive through a covered bridge over the trout

stream and past sheep grazing behind aged Tennessee cedar rail fencing. The approach and arrival sequence practically sings the tune "Over the river and through the woods to grandmother's house we go," especially as you pass a simple white chapel with spire and wildflowers.

After following the trout stream racing beside the drive, a pocket of sun ahead indicates a meadow nestled between high mossy

BELOW AND RIGHT:
Toad Hall sits adjacent an
atmospheric lake formed
from old trout ponds.
Turkey sculptures enliven
the island.

boulder cliffs and mature mountain woodland. Here is the epicenter of Toad Hall; a place
where turkeys, trout and family coexist. This
bottomland was once a small trout hatchery
with three irregularly shaped ponds sans trout
and ripe with mosquitoes. The ponds morphed
into a picturesque pond complete with tulip
poplar island and fed with fresh water from the
adjacent stream. Weeping willows along the
lakeside accent the log guest cottage with its
wooden outhouse with crescent moon on the
door. A pirates' ship shuttles young Tom Saw-
yers and Huck Finns over to the island to complete the picture of a simple, outdoor life filled
with adventures.

The log cabin vista across the lake is viewed
from Toad Hall, a gracious two-story log cabin
designed by Jack Davis, an architect from
Atlanta, Georgia. Built by Hickory Construction of Knoxville, the house is a masterpiece of
merging form and function all wrapped up in
period materials. Not an amenity is overlooked
and everything blends into a distinctive mix of
comfort, luxury and peace.

The approach to the house is along a crunchy,
gravel courtyard framed on four sides by the
barn and stone shed, with Toad Hall seen on
axis through the dogtrot barn. Large flat crab
orchard stones pave the way across the grassy
forecourt past mature, billowing boxwoods
that frame the simple lawn. Boxwoods anchor
the house and form hedges to separate functional areas from the appreciation of nature.

The garden shed and kitchen garden occupy the right side of Toad Hall and enjoy full sun opening onto the lake lawn. Mature tulip poplars backdrop the shed and old-fashioned varieties of hydrangea and antique roses weave in and out of the picture. The centerpiece kitchen garden is based on an eighteenth-century pattern of four parts, the oldest garden known to mankind. Espalier pears and apples provide a low cordon hedge as edible perimeter fencing. Kingsville boxwoods, a dwarf form of edging boxwood, trim out the four parts and prostrate rosemary mixed with lavender subdues the circle in the center. The understated grass and stepping-stone paths echo Toad Hall's simple, natural lifestyle and knit this garden into the surrounding landscape.

LEFT: A terrace with a view overlooking Silver Slip in Wade Hampton, Cashiers, North Carolina, provides the Linda and Dick Cravey family with multipurpose space for grandchildren.

LOWER: A terrace is often a frame of mind. For Kate and Bruce Knauft, a social outing on their deck is integral to their love of European travel. Although their dining area is really a deck, we always refer to it as "the terrace."

TERRACE

A flat area, integral with the earth and surfaced with stone, brick, gravel or grass, this is the most adaptable type of space.

Terraces are an essential kit and can extend 8 x 8 feet, 12 x 18 feet, 20 x 24 feet, etc., to provide seating or dining for varying sizes and can interlock with garden space between. The antique slabs of marble, previously used as paving in Rome, have been well worn by the scrapes of chairs over time. Bluestone, crab orchard, limestone or brick are also great choices.

CHAPTER 3

Be Active

Active outdoor pursuits took man into nature from the beginning of time. In lifelong landscapes, areas for activities, such as Pilates, yoga, rebounding, swimming and playing, are created. Active recreation takes on a whole new meaning when gardening is considered. Clipping hedges, mulching, walking up and down hills and pushing carts are great exercise.

Active recreational spaces can be as small as 8 x 8 feet (16 square feet) for yoga or Pilates. Large swimming pools can require 40 x 60 feet (2,400 square feet). Children need active, interpretive play areas designed to encourage connection with nature plus include observation and connection with their families.

What outdoor activity is more varied and rewarding than puttering around tending, planting, picking and sharing your garden? So many garden areas can be designed to offer continuous pleasure: streams, fountains and ponds, vegetables, soft fruit and orchards, kitchen gardens, a flower patch, a perennial sweep, herb gardens, woodland walks, collections of bonsai, or simply potted plants on a balcony.

Given this candy box of choices, hold foremost in your mind that gardens are living entities. Like a double-sided coin, gardens are always evolving and morphing into something inspirational, or they can become your worst nightmare during drought or pestilence. Managing the needs of a garden may not be entirely evident at first.

A garden needs a support system. In our family garden patch, I am the caregiver who searches out pests, sprays, dusts, ties up vines and processes the produce. My husband, Hugh, has a calling to be the person who fertilizes with organic bits and compost tea. He is the best weeder in the world. We plant, harvest and pluck spent leaves

Croquet is becoming increasingly popular as a sport in the United States. In Highlands, North Carolina, more than 250 people vie for spots to play a game at this mountain retreat.

property is a bit of work but pays lavish dividends in the future. Gardens delight the senses or may stand alone as gardens to be enjoyed from a balcony or window. So be active and hone your material, and it will reward you in many ways.

I like to think that gardeners live longer. It must be the great air and exercise that serves the body and soul. The benefits of being active outside are manifold: deeper breath work, looser muscles, stress reduction, vitamin D from the sun, all ages can participate and gardening activities can affect a shift in your mental place.

Be careful in a garden. Balance and center yourself before going to work. Use the right tool for the job, such as ergonomic trowels and spades, plus clothing with lots of pockets, such as a garden apron. I walk around armed for what looks like combat in my garden, with clippers hanging and twine following me around.

Making the garden a place for exercise takes on another mind-set. We added a Pilates bench and love it for stretching before and after work. A rebounder sits on a pad of grass and invites a bounce in between tasks, which is fun. Aerobic exercises such as stair climbing are appropriate to our slopes while carrying wood to the shed. The adrenalin and endorphin releases that come from aerobic exercise help my mood when the serotonin and dopamine kick into play. Balance is improved as your core musculature is strengthened. We recommend designing fitness goals into your garden.

like chickens searching for a juicy bug. Therefore, choose the style and size of your garden so that you can enjoy the reality of being its companion.

This book considers that garden destinations are part of your four-part master plan and walkways provide access. Thoughtful consideration of garden interconnections with the rest of the

Lifelong Landscape Patterns and Places:
KITCHEN GARDEN

A kitchen garden is the quintessential collection of man's favorite plants for sustenance, medicine and delight. A classic kitchen garden is a pattern with four pathways and a central circle surrounded by a tall wall. We use bumps of variegated boxwoods to anchor corners of beds. A frill of Kingsville dwarf boxwoods lines the perimeter of each of the four central beds for winter armature.

In my kitchen garden, twenty-two espaliered apple and pear trees line the perimeter like a living fence. Interior beds harbor seasonal vegetables, while the perimeter burgeons with beds of chard, kale, comfrey and asparagus. Lettuces flit here and there, mixing with mustards and the odd borage. Root vegetables, the most stable citizens of the garden, have their own compartments.

Kitchen gardens are quite customizable. At Highcote, cast-iron gypsy kettles anchor the entry and are planted with thyme and chives. Benches settle into useful corners for placing baskets or tools. A birdhouse gourd tree rules the sky above the garden in hopes of fostering a martin colony. We ponder adding a bee house or two, and maybe chickens are coming here to live next spring. This is becoming a mini-farm and only occupies a space of 7,200 square feet (60 x 20 feet).

A raised bed helps to promote drainage, so we use a 12 x 2-inch edging board, with six inches showing aboveground, and six inches below to hold the beds. Bricks or stone set without mortar are preferable. To green up the garden in winter, use an evergreen planting of squatty boxwoods, parsley or chives. Less formal edges include lettuces or herbs, or nasturtiums are happy cascading over the edges to mingle with the walk.

Our garden at Highcote
is way too much fun in
the summer when we
stake the tomatoes and
pull the weeds. Just
harvesting leaves of kale
is a great way to get into
the fresh air and collect a
healthy meal for any age.

A Charming
Kitchen Garden

THIS ODD-SHAPED AREA
at Ushuata was almost a
heartbreaker. The targeted
garden area is underpinned
with a river of conduits
that service the house.
The plateau retaining wall
angles off at an odd direction, leaving us a leftover
space. By mapping the

existing structures and adding functional needs, such as
access to the lower grounds
on the grass path beyond,
an enclosed space was created. By spraying the pro-
posed garden bed outlines
on the ground, adjustments
were made to balance the
kitchen garden pattern.

Lifelong
Landscape
ACTIVITIES

For more active landscape patterns, visit www.
dargan.com/landscapeyourlife. My favorite pool
design is a curved shape with a diagonal line forty
feet long for swimming laps. The pool has a van-
ishing edge that takes in the woodland view at the
curved end. The water is non-chlorinated, there
are places to sit in water and relax in conversation.
The sides are a dove gray color of plaster and the
resultant water color is a medium cobalt blue. The
paving around the pool is stepping-stones set with
ground covers between for a soft interface. This is
the pool of my dreams. Did I mention the spa?

ABOVE: A splash of water enlivens this pool courtyard in New Orleans. Comfortable seating, relaxing sound and covered dining makes the Heebe pool a winner.

RIGHT: The Pearl River offers a magnificent backdrop to the spa and lake at this family retreat.

A Gracious Stroll Garden

IN AUGUSTA, Georgia, a series of destinations entice a wander around these eight acres of mature Georgia landscape. Featuring a summerhouse, large formal flower garden, a woodland walk, camellia collection, and Asian garden, this house and garden are lovingly maintained by Nola and Charles Falcone. There are many active and passive places for retreats and refuge beneath the shelter of the towering pines and magnolias. Hugh Dargan worked closely with Nola in designing the series of woodland walks.

Question: How did you decide where to place the walks?

Dargan: "We walked through the existing trees and imagined how I could lay out a continuously curving series of paths that created enough depth in planting areas to accommodate her camellia collection and distance between the paths themselves. From the tree survey, I laid it out on paper so it could be installed properly. Her camellia collection, as far as I know, contains the largest collection of camellia varieties in a private garden in the South and now numbers more than 150 varieties."

Question: How did you work with the existing pattern garden?

Dargan: "The crosswalks were there with the square, and we added the perimeter walks to complete the four-square pattern. It really is supposed to be a collection of southern perennials. For parties, it can be ramped up a bit by adding delphiniums and foxgloves, but after the end of May, it goes to sleep. It is terribly hot in Augusta in the summer."

Question: How is the maintenance of this large garden managed?

Dargan: "Nola is very active in gardening. She directs the planting, mulching, weeding, mowing and tending. She loves her formal garden and is personally involved with planting seasonal flowers and tending perennials, especially her daylily collection. There are many collections and opportunity to divide and rearrange plants. This is both an active garden and a passive one, for there are plenty of shady benches and leisurely walkways to enjoy simply being outside."

RIGHT: Formal flower gardens are tough to maintain. A balanced collection of plants inevitably gives way to unequal shading and root competition, funny wet spots or, worst yet, voles. So, a periodic facelift is generally required. Maybe the best approach is to go for one season, a burst of controlled color and be amazed, then let it slumber the rest of the year.

Why Gardening Is an Important ACTIVITY

Activity in the garden leads to many benefits including stronger bones, self-assurance, stress reduction and balance. A garden "Trim Trail," popular in England, has stations available to do leg stretches and pushups. Pilates and rebounding are popular in America as compact, easy ways to insert alternate exercise into your lifestyle. Gardeners seem to live longer, healthier lives, so loosen up before going out to prune, and stretch when you finish to ensure you enjoy gardening in the future.

STRETCHING

Just like any workout, one needs a chance to decompress after doing gardening activities. The best way to lessen post-exercise stiffness and protect muscles from injury is stretching prior to any workout. Take a few minutes to stretch before or after your gardening session, and you'll find your muscles and bones appreciate it in days to come. Stretching works by lengthening muscles and reducing tightness in them.

Some of my favorite stretches include leg lengthening, hip loosening, thigh stretching, side stretching and upper arm stretching. Each of these is pretty self-explanatory and can become part of your garden fitness regime.

I am bad at charging into tasks, so remember to pace yourself. If you ever feel short of breath, dizzy or faint, stop and rest. Cease activity if you feel pain. I try to change positions regularly in order to avoid stiffness. A hat is useful. In the garden, I always carry a bottle of water; if not to drink, to throw at a squirrel or rabbit.

GARDENING AS A CALORIE BUSTER

Activities in gardens combined with horticultural pursuits are great calorie burners. Did you know that an average-sized person who carries heavy loads, such as wood, burns from 450 to 700 calories an hour? Chopping and splitting can burn 325 calories per hour, weeding and raking grass hover around 225 to 260 calories per hour, while watering your plants is only 90 calories per hour.

The magnificent and serene backdrop of Linda and Dick Cravey's home in Wade Hampton located in Cashiers, North Carolina, is punctuated by their ethereal garden sculpture.

CHAPTER 4

Passive Places

Passive recreation design, such as places for prayer, meditation, reading, playing music, massage or sunning, takes little room and is scaled to the needs of the static human figure. Viewing a formal garden pattern, relaxing in a swing, walking a labyrinth or listening to a fountain are considered passive recreation.

In some ways, passive recreation spaces are more difficult to design than active ones. The complex methods employed to awaken the five senses in a very small space, such as a balcony, small terrace or courtyard, challenge you to think outside the box. Just sitting and breathing takes nine square feet (3 x 3 space).

The courtyard garden of Judy and the late Lawrence Walz has all the right components for a passive retreat: koi pond, shady arbor, raised garden beds and interesting paving.

Inspiration, Rejuvenation, and Stress REDUCERS

So, a space that encourages passive recreation is one that is quiet, peaceful and oftentimes set aside from the busiest areas. Whether it is your intent to reflect on your day or simply to enjoy nature, these areas are sure to help you in your peaceful pursuits. Children need downtime, and a shady place with a jigsaw puzzle or a paint kit works wonders to calm a busy child. The two-person household and elders share similar needs such as desire for sun pockets, shady places to sit, and a new garden fountain to mask off-site sounds and to add ambient calm.

PROJECT FILE
A Serene Courtyard Garden

AT JUDY WALZ'S home in Atlanta, a fine perimeter courtyard was designed to accommodate a linkage between kitchen and dining room. A large arbor, fishpond and garden beds complete the picture. This garden excels in passive places. A shady place to read a good book and a place to sit and watch fish move lazily around make it relaxing for three generations. The pretty curved series of beds, built of aged building materials, offers lines of beauty that relax the eye and promote stress relief.

Lifelong
Landscape
Patterns
AND PLACES

CHAISE LOUNGE

A comfortable place to sit is essential in passive places. The chaise lounge is the classic forum that functions well for the human body.

LABYRINTH

A quiet time walking in a slow curvilinear line produces a Zen-like state and can stimulate inspiration. Historically, labyrinths connected man to god in patterns on cathedral floors.

PARTERRES AND VIEW GARDENS

Parterres are commonly found in formal gardens and consist of tightly clipped hedges that are frequently in symmetrical patterns and have ornate designs. Versailles in Paris, Kensington Palace in London, and Villa Lante in Bagnaia, Italy, are all known for their spectacular boxwood parterres.

SCULPTURE

Choose your sculpture wisely. A size that is three-quarters actual is appropriate to figurative works; smaller can be dangerously out of scale. My favorite is mossy limestone, easily created in adding moss, yogurt, olive oil and corn syrup to new statues.

FACING LEFT: At Pashley House in England, this gardener statue greets guests in the kitchen garden.

ABOVE: A treasured visit home is punctuated by a quiet read in this restful spot beneath the arbor at the Walt Home.

LEFT: In Sea Island, Georgia, the grass labyrinth is based on medieval patterns and is situated in a quiet view area adjacent to the cloister spa.

Thinking
Passively to
Refresh the Body
AND SOUL

A porch swing set with comfortable pillows provides a place for relaxation at Kayrita and Hal Anderson's home in Buckhead in Atlanta, Georgia.

In passive places, retreats to rejuvenate the body and soul predominate the landscape of people's dreams. Many of these places, such as pattern gardens, are designed to promote a feeling of calm by using repeated forms and green to sooth the onlooker. Please remember, they need maintenance. When planning your passive place, be sure to balance the needs versus your pleasure to keep it looking calm.

SWING
Our favorite swings hang from arbors or trees where you are semi-covered with greenery. A long, interesting view enhances the experience.

The formal garden at The Wortham House Bed and Breakfast features topiaries preened by Gene Johnson at 54 Montage Street in Charleston, South Carolina. (Photo by Louisa Pringe Cameron)

PROJECT FILE

The Pleasure Parterre

FALLING IN LOVE with a piece of architectural history is a recipe for success when Gene and Betsy Johnson get their juices flowing. Part home, part bed and breakfast, this landscape enjoys the luxury of space in historic Charleston, South Carolina. They even have a Gothic potting shed.

Question: What was the property like when you first saw it?

Gene: "The rear half of the house was gone with tar paper and four fireplaces looming. Formica, trash everywhere and a horrible chain-link fence on the rear property line made us think we'd lost our minds, plus all that was left of the original kitchen house was the chimney remains."

Question: How do you design a passive retreat if there is no garden?

Gene: "Well, all we had was a large palmetto, a

huge holly and a 200-year-old oak, which died soon after construction left the garden in blazing sunlight. So we started the garden to return a spirit of place to this wasteland. First the new Kwansan cherries began to die. This taught us to roll with the punches, just like in life, since you don't know what will happen, and just sort of mend yourself."

Johnson went on to create a utopia that includes a large parterre garden, series of linkage gardens to the bed and breakfast guesthouse, and the retreat where the old live oak once stood tall.

Question: How did Gene decide to begin?

Gene: "From the back to the front, which makes sense. We started in front of the carriage house and proceeded to the four-part garden. I've always wanted a wonderful evergreen

garden. In the middle of the parterre, I started with a parallel box lined with hibiscus and laurel bay standards."

Question: How did you choose the pattern?

Gene: "Well I thought I invented it, but now I know it is the international symbol for garden! It is a pattern garden. Formal is not the proper word for its design, which implies stiffness and reserve. It is southern and doesn't age. Every time you look at it, it is quiet. The color inside the parterres is green, because I am not good with color."

Question: How about your family and grandchildren; how do they use the garden?

Gene: "Oh, they make do and they wander around looking at the garden. I didn't want a place to play ball after they left home."

WALL FOUNTAIN

In small spaces, wall-mounted fountains perform beautifully without crowding a seating area. Scale is everything. A small wall-mounted fountain need not have a shell much deeper than eight inches and a surround of twenty-four inches high, and a basin to catch the outflow of no more than eighteen inches. In designing backdrop fountain features, a scale model, cut from newspaper and tacked to the wall, is very helpful.

So much is to be considered in building a fountain. How to run the recirculating pipe through the wall is a challenge for mounted fountains.

If your fountain basin calls for greenery, remember the golden rule: 70 percent water surface coverage above or below the surface. If the fountain has a feature, use plants with a diversity of heights to frame the feature.

FACING UPPER: The Tree of Life fountain at Hugh and Jane McCall's courtyard in Charlotte brings a quiet background sound to the busy area.

FACING LOWER: The O'Leary fountain is situated adjacent the courtyard and provides small background sound that is relaxing. Many water plants thrive in fountain environments.

Lifelong Landscape Activities

Chi Gong
Meditation
Pilates
Yoga

For more examples of passive landscape patterns, visit www.dargan/landscapeyourlife.com.

UPPER LEFT: Chi gong, an ancient Eastern longevity practice, is simple to learn and enhances all parts of your body, including digestion and memory.

UPPER RIGHT: Meditation offers access to a centered life and a great place to recharge your batteries after a hectic day.

This stepping-stone
walk along a bed edge
provides for dry feet in
the Valenta garden in
Cashiers, North Carolina.

CHAPTER 5

Freedom of Access & Choice

Access to, from and around your landscape is vital for use, delight and health. Both access and enclosure systems are integral parts of lifelong landscapes. These systems are dynamic patterns and include nodes, pot ears, gates, fences, walls, steps, or solid or soft walks. Pathways, shaped by plant materials like the allee, loosely hedged paths, Zen walkways or shrub nodes make access to the garden healthy, fun and serviceable.

Functional access systems are critical to all users. A circular path around the property that takes in the front and the back is a classic design with no dead ends and is convenient for service. Many children on tricycles love to go around and around a circular pathway through small beds of plantings and alongside grass or a terrace. Elders, especially those living in apartments or restricted spaces, relish the opportunity to walk where they wish with assistance or under their own power. If freedom of access is controlled by gates such as in townhomes, gardens with pets, or advanced medical facilities, inner loops are a must for motility within the system. Alzheimer patients readily get confused when

The long walk at Timberline is punctuated with a granite birdbath and large tub for lotus. Variegated hostas and ferns interspersed with Japanese maples and ladies mantle keep the eye entertained.

Appeal
to Your SENSE
of Well-Being

they encounter a dead end or cross-axis; circular paths are very stress-reducing for this user group.

The benefit of access and exercise are manifold. Endorphin levels, which promote happiness and pain reduction, are elevated after exercise. Being outside reduces stress by dropping cortisol levels and accesses healthy sunlight for Vitamin D.

The idea of walking, even on a circular path, will metaphorically take you away from your troubles. Creating a place to do chi gong, yoga or Pilates for breath work and stretching will oxygenate your blood and increase cellular health. Those minimally active places are typically 8 x 8 feet to fit the human body, when stretched finger tip to toe.

A wide, level walking surface is great for elders; stepping-stones set into grass work well for most adults and child's play. Design to meet your needs. A typical path is five feet wide, but if you are moving triplets in a baby carriage or handling a wheelchair, think again and measure your vehicle. Always consider the use of permeable surfaces to help Mother Nature recharge the groundwater supply. Creating a flat area where there is none, such as grass or terraced slopes on hillsides, is a functional consideration and part of a master plan. Lighting is a critical part of extending access and use of the garden at night.

Lifelong Landscape
PATTERNS AND PLACES

ALLEE

Using an allee of trees is a beautiful way to line long driveways or roads and make the home, or hub, the focal point of the drive: with hundred-year-old oaks or freshly planted maple saplings, an allee is a great addition to any drive and is sure to be beautiful.

THE CIRCULAR WALK

In designing any garden, a looped perambulation is essential to maintenance and pleasure. Begin at a gate or terrace, wander around, experience various garden moments, then exit in one fluid moment. Paths that reverse upon themselves need at least a modest tear drop at the terminus to divorce one's self from the previous direction. A bench at a turning point along a short directional path is a great place to pause. The benefit of a circular path is also for children who can go round and round to burn off energy. Alzheimer patients prefer this form of garden experience and are encouraged to return to exercise. A circular path may be of brick, stepping-stones, wood chips or simply grass.

FENCE

A wooden fence can vary in height from twenty-four inches to keep a toddler or small child inside, or five or six feet for enclosing livestock or security. We often use a thirty-six-inch roll of hardware cloth, chicken or hog wire fence installed twelve inches deep in the ground to repel voles and suspend the upper twenty-four inches between unpainted, treated wooden posts. A double row of mixed shrubs is planted on either side to hide the wire structure. This is far preferable to chain-link fencing and will contain most active inmates.

GATE

Enclosures require entry points for security. The design of a gate can be as fanciful as your dreams. Gates are generally three to five feet wide for walking guests and twelve feet at drives.

LEFT: This circular walk at Margaret and Warren Wills' house in Cashiers at Wade Hampton curves gently from the driveway to the front door along natural paving stones and stepping-slab steps.

RIGHT: Drs. Russell Holiday and Hal Cottingham enjoy access to their precious flower garden along stepping-stones with blue trailing lobelia planted between the cracks.

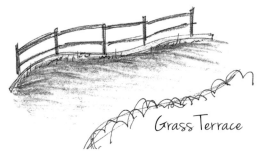

Grass Terrace

ABOVE: This British grass terrace cut into a pasture features a rough-cut border of meadow wildflowers.

RIGHT: In the McIntyre's Charleston garden, a clipped hedge of Kingsville boxwood frames the garden beds.

GRASS TERRACES

The grass terrace is different from the *tapis vert* as it is not a geometric size and shape. It is the result of building a flat area on a sloping lot and requires a retaining wall. A successful, small grass terrace is bordered with a three-foot width of planting to protect the edge and is at least eight feet wide. I find grass terraces extremely useful for walking pets, creating a small vignette outside a window, a seating area, an adjunct dining space or a utility area for compost. An undulating border provides interest and stepping-stones along the edge improves visual design and usefulness.

HEDGES

Hedges offer containment along grass terraces or pathways. Scale is important and an overgrown hedge will overpower its surroundings.

BELOW: Intersecting paths at Thuja Gardens in Asticou, Maine, feature a large node framed by mosses.

RIGHT: A gracious front landing complete with welcoming bench presents a friendly approach at the Clements residence in Jacksonville, Florida.

LANDING

The landing is the welcoming threshold to your home. Make it gracious, at least eight feet wide and made of high-quality materials.

NODE

A node is a place of decision. Do you want to go right, left, north or south? Often nodes employ focal points for way-finding in the landscape. It refers to a winding path with views sculpted into "set pieces," or a larger sphere of view to a distant feature, researched by an atmospheric path. Light and shadow play a large role in creating a sense of space and forward motion. You go from one view (light) through shade (dark) to the next pool of light. Nodes are typically half the size of a path if they include pot ears.

Lighting:
Delight in
the Night

NIGHT LIGHTING for accent is a specialty in our garden at Highcote. We've experimented with every manner of lighting fixture, from coffee cans with holes punched into the sides to frosted milk bottles. Virtually anything can be wired with low-voltage wire and a small bulb. A specialist can provide an enormous amount of input for long-term and short-term fixture locations, wiring plan, transformers and timer.

We tend to use lighting high in trees very sparingly due to preference for source illumination. In hard-to-light areas, ceilings of structures like pavilions, or arbors, bullet lights fixed with pink filters cast soft, natural light. We always use the lowest wattage possible, such as a 9- or 12-volt bulb, and once your eyes are accustomed to being outside, little light is needed to highlight paths. For a realistic effect of candlelight in an old miner's lantern or glass globe, use theater frost spray or candle wax smoke and let it be misty. I never clean my globes.

ABOVE: A bottle light adds interest to the landscape at Highcote.

LEFT AND FACING: Timberline's terrace steps are illuminated with clamshell copper lights by The Outdoor Lights.

Shrub nodes are often defined with
boxwood families for a dad, mother and
baby boxwood collection for height interest.

Boxwood Nodes

RIGHT: Pot ears frame
the entrance to the Wills'
walk-in in Buckhead.

Pot Ears

POT EARS

Pot ears are useful in many ways, both aesthetically and functionally. They help denote the beginning of a path, the entry to a house or are used as an anchor to thresholds. Often a slab of stone or rock, "pot ears" are perfect for potted plants that add color to your landscape. The typical size of pot ear is 18 x 18 inches or 24 x 24 inches for larger vessels.

SHRUB NODE

A node is often defined by graduated sizes of plant materials such as 12-, 24- and 36-inch plants on either side to provide a sense of enclosure.

SOFT WALKS

Stones should be laid directly on the earth with a one-inch crack between each. Allow

LEFT: Blickling, a National Trust property in England, uses shrub nodes to announce the formal garden.

BELOW: A tapestry of stepables colonizes this walkway consisting of alchemilla, creeping jenny and laurentia.

grass, moss and small flowers to grow in these cracks. No cement or mortar is necessary.

There are multiple benefits in this natural way of paving. The stones do not crack as the earth settles, it helps preserve delicate ecological areas, and it helps unite the space with the environment. Soft walks are great for meandering pathways from one garden room to another or within the garden itself.

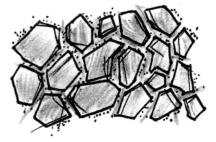

Paving with Cracks between Stones

BELOW: Solid walkways offer stable footing for all ages. At Nancy and Holcombe Green's Wade Hampton house in Cashiers, frequent rains dictate dry footing to reach the front door.

SOLID WALKS

Solid walks are pathways made of stone, brick or any type of material that is bonded together by mortar or grout. Solid walks are perfect for walks to doorways or areas where people need to be directed. A path for two people is five feet wide, and a single person needs twenty-four to twenty-six inches.

TERRACED SLOPE

Terraces benefit the land by controlling erosion. They slow down water and prevent rills by spreading water more evenly. Terraces should tie into the building edge and relate to the general presentation of the property. Terracing creates a micro-system of draining and protects topsoil.

STEPS

Steps are access points and require careful consideration. Materials such as natural stone, brick

LEFT: The Governor's Palace kitchen garden in Colonial Williamsburg has descending terraces evenly spaced for drainage and vegetable production.

BELOW: Steps lead to the arbor walk at the Ruthie and Berryman Edwards residence in Highlands, North Carolina.

and bluestone work well for structured steps, while black locust logs and grass ramps provide casual access. The tread riser relationship of twelve-inch tread with six-inch riser is a classic formula for comfortable steps. Be sure to allow a landing after runs of six to eight steps to allow for a breather, provide a bench for rest, and then start the next set of steps. Otherwise, a long tongue of steps navigating a steep hill is daunting to even the most agile mountain goat or visitor.

Terraced Slope

WHEELCHAIR ACCESS

What better way to welcome universal access needs for a baby stroller or wheelchair than a nice wide walkway? When set with raised beds conveniently cantilevered for gardening activities, this access system offers access to healthy outdoor pursuits.

WALLS FOR PRIVACY

Enclosures for courtyards and along townhouse property lines are built of wood panels or masonry. Zoning regulations dictate the height of these enclosures, so know your local ordinances. Walls are often designed to harmonize with the house and blend into the domestic landscape, offering places to hang wall fountains or create a backdrop focal point.

Conveniently
Wandering
AROUND

Choices and access is a large topic that is integral to all-age enjoyment of our gardens. Landscape patterns as diverse as paths, gates, soft walks, circular walks, wheelchair access, nodes, pot ears and steps are all clearly functional. The amount of detail to design and build these features ranges from exquisite to hardware store solutions and every imaginable expression in between. To express your personality, feel free to experiment with materials and artistic expressions of these surfaces. Just be sure to check your local zoning codes for setbacks and enclosure heights.

LEFT: The Chicago Botanic Garden's Therapy Garden provides multiple venues for universal access to explore and enjoy being outdoors. It excels at interpretation and practical application of lifelong landscape design techniques.

BELOW: In Cecile and Phil McCaull's garden in Highlands, a fountain invites a visit.

CHAPTER 6

Activate Your Senses to Reduce Stress

110

Stress is an enormous contributing factor in your lifelong health. Your landscape can easily be designed to provide quick remedies for meeting the challenges of everyday life. In a garden environment, the benefits of stress-reducing activities range from lowering blood pressure to reducing cortisol levels. Endorphins, the feel-good hormones produced by your body, are often released in relaxing environments and may even reduce need for pain medication.

Our daily patterns define our lifestyles and are unique. Whether it is getting your life in order before work, doing a myriad of family errands, finding personal time, or coping with limited motility and energy, each stage of life has daily stressors. Your body reacts to stress by raising the cortisol level in your blood. This physiological process has a domino effect on your body; over time, it contributes to aging, and thus the quality of your life. While this book does not intend to treat individual stress cases and causes, it is important to understand how your reaction to sustained stress works and its long-term health implications. With this knowledge, you are better informed to design a stress-busting environment.

FACING: Chester the labradoodle enjoys a romp in the hostas to play peek-a-boo with owners Peggy and J. F. Bryax.

Evidence-based research shows that both pain medication and cortisol levels (the stress hormone) are reduced when people visit gardens. The type of garden varies. Densely planted pathways that encourage intimate contact by brushing up against plants show the highest stress-reduction indices. Deep breathing by walking or meditating in a garden opens your chest and airways, allowing oxygen into your blood. This oxygen helps remove toxins, gradually equalizing blood pressure, lowering cortisol and calming the nerves. A change in elevation, a distant vista, viewing sculpture or relaxing in an enclosed, green refuge can affect a change in your attitude that takes you outside of yourself and promotes both mental and physical health.

Animals
Reduce
Stress

Pets in a garden, such as dogs, cats and birds, bring comfort and companionship to all groups of lifelong landscape dwellers. Feeding stations, for example, designed to draw a variety of bird types, are popular due to the diverse activity of birdlife generated. Keep your feeders well stocked and the birds will flock to the table. My favorite is a thistle sock for gold finches. Birdhouses are amazing places, especially in urban areas. They are soon colonized by sparrows or house wrens. Put one up and see what happens. Similar to watching chickens, bird watching is an endless joy.

ABOVE: Barbara Graham from Columbia, South Carolina, enjoys a visit with a cat at a friend's bee farm.

It is widely known that pets, particularly cats and dogs, enhance the physical, social, emotional and cognitive condition of a person. Pet therapy is great for rehabilitation of children and depressed or lonely adults. The unconditional love of a pet as a constant companion is comforting, lifts the spirits and gives many reasons to get up in the morning.

All said, pets need places in the landscape to refresh themselves as much as humans. A dog or cat garden can be as small as a 5 x 5-foot space.

A small three-foot hedge or low lattice wall will remove it from everyday sight. Dogs can easily be trained to use this patch of grass or ground cover for their daily business, while cats will always gravitate toward a kitty litter box, which can be placed in a shelter. Be sure to clean up after your pet and dispose of waste properly. Neither dog nor cat refuse has much value as a fertilizer but does offer potential health hazards, so composting is not recommended.

FACING: Chickens, especially quail bantams, make wonderful pets, are fun to watch and produce eggs as well. A typical chicken coop is 12 x 12 feet square and needs shade, water and protection on all sides, including the bottom, from foxes.

Defining Stress

ABOVE: A birdbath placed as a mini-destination along a shrub boarder provides visual stimulation on a curved walk.

A LIFELONG landscape with places for stress reduction is but one step toward radiant health; we need to de-stress our inner bodies as well. Many of us grew up eating processed foods, living with environmental toxins and now have compromised immune and digestive systems. It is prudent to treat the inner self as well as create a supportive outdoor environment.

Donna Gates, a pioneer in body ecology, outlines steps for rejuvenating and nourishing your body. From detoxification and alkalizing your body to eating densely nutritious foods and practicing stress-reduction bodywork, Donna addresses the process to regain balance in your lifestyle, especially with regard to the inner body. Because this process includes organic food sources AND activities, you can design supportive places in your lifelong landscape to include an organic home vegetable garden or sunbathing pocket to practice activities such as chi gong, yoga and breath work.

BELOW: At Thuja Gardens in Asticou, Maine, a riot of well-planned color sets the senses on fire in this totally organic garden.

RIGHT: Our Red-Hot Mama border in high gear in mid-July is ready for a party.

Perennial Flower Gardens

The most requested garden is the low-maintenance, perennial flower garden. Bulletproof combinations are possible and my best advice is to start small. Choose plant clumps of at least three to five plants of your favorite species. A manageable sweep is between five and eight feet deep and twenty feet long. A boxwood or other evergreen bump to anchor the ends provides edge definition. When standing five to eight feet from a garden, the human eye can view about twenty feet at a time. If you are colonizing a really long border, break it into sections with an evergreen. The British do this very skillfully with evergreen buttresses and boxwoods.

A successful perennial sweep has a three-dimensional profile. It starts low at the front edges, rises to about eighteen inches, and then gets taller at the back. For example, having dianthus at the

front, backed by daylilies, sedum "autumn joy," and iris, provides varying heights and textures. Try for interest in every season and do not be afraid to allow annuals to self-seed. I love lychnis, stick verbena and Queen Anne's lace coming up in my beds. Use annuals to pump up slack times by saving out areas for them in the front along edges, such as trailing lobelia, or heat-loving annuals in the rear that take time to grow.

Color blending usually works best if you follow a color wheel and place complementary colors next to one another, which are opposites on the color wheel. I always like to drop in a sixth of pale yellow in gardens filled with reds and lavenders, and switch to using whites in similar proportion when blending blue gardens. The small amount of light color makes the darker colors nearby "pop."

The "snail's trail" at Timberline is a mini-labyrinth. It starts with a millstone and winds in a circle of ever-larger stones before setting off across the woodland to end in the circular seating area by the house.

Textures and Patterns

A simple path of bark chips, leaves or moss provides a cushioned surface underfoot. A woodland walk, especially a new walk, needs time to grow a patina and encourage plants to intermingle with the edges. Plants growing wild along the sides, within the confines of nature, will delight the eye with variable textures, leaf patterns, plant forms and fruit color. The interplay of this tapestry of plants is tremendously stress reducing and a proven aid in the healing process.

BELOW: The Dowden cascade and bridge create a refreshing vista beside a small lake.

RIGHT: Mimicking a stream or waterfall is not easy, but Bob Dews from Cashiers makes it look easy with moss, water plants and native materials placed in a realistic fashion.

WATERFALLS

A babbling cascade along a mossy, narrow tributary while hiking convinced me I should have something like it to enjoy every day. Because most man-made waterfalls look forced, I go for a narrow cascade with ferns hanging over sides and mossy boulders set with shelves. River rocks of various size and color lining the bottom and sides help add to the natural feel. The smaller the cascade the better, tapering from eighteen to twenty-four inches at the top to a realistic thirty-six inches at the base for perspective. Ideally, the collection pond at the bottom need not be more than forty-eight inches wide and no more than thirty-six inches deep. A layered vegetated backdrop is of utmost importance.

When designing a waterfall, it is all about the sound. I suggest that if clients want a series of falls, they have separate pumps for each waterfall. This enables management of repairs in a timely fashion.

Initially fill your waterfall by hand with a hose and watch the water level and cascade shape. Like most water features, you need electricity nearby for the pump. A sump pump is an amazingly versatile, durable and inexpensive piece of equipment. It provides a good strong flow of water at the cascade. Just drop it into your basin after converting the outflow to work with garden hose or two-foot flexible pile. Then work the pipe under some rocks and branches, and enjoy a babbling brook.

The rear watershed of our property sits adjacent to our dining pavilion and slopes gently down

LOWER: A relaxing swim followed by a massage or sauna is a great way to de-stress. This Palm Beach home has a bonus of swan decoys to scare away raccoons and other varmints who also enjoy a swim.

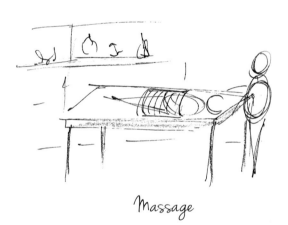

Massage

from the woodland. It was so perfect for a small waterfall that we were chomping at the bit to hire strong backs; rocks are very heavy. It is important that the watercourse be set with shelves of flat stone to create a cascade effect, but not look hokey. Let a photograph of a natural fall be your guide. Ferns and allied wetland plantings such as mosses and sedges are beautiful to colonize the sides, but you need to plant them and make a place for others to join. A bonus to our waterfall was a native milkweed, *Asclepias exalta,* which volunteered and flourished, providing a charming fireworks display of cascading red and white flowers and enormous seed pods.

Saunas and Spas

When we decided to install a far-infrared sauna in our potting shed, it was part luxury item and part health equipment. The benefits of a far-infrared sauna are legion and clinical data shows high blood pressure reduction, increased core temperature, detoxification, weight loss, skin rejuvenation, relaxation and post-workout muscle recovery. When used in combination with a cold-plunge pool and heated spa, the immune system is stimulated.

A typical one-person sauna is about forty-eight inches wide and thirty-six inches deep. We prefer far-infrared saunas because they promote perspiration without making you feel terribly hot, as do traditional hot rocks and wood-fired moist saunas. However, these are electrically powered and need to be housed in a shelter. The skin is the largest detoxifying organ in the body and the sauna promotes perspiration, which makes a convenient outdoor shower particularly desirable.

Nothing evokes relaxation like a spa moment in a natural basin outside. Spas can be constructed of stone, be self-contained in a wooden tub or be ordered as a plastic form for in-ground use. Hot water and massage jets are operated by a pump generally housed adjacent to the spa. Spas are often associated with swimming pools and located at the end closest to the pool house.

Sizes of spas vary, but the most efficient ones are approximately five to six feet across and can seat two people. They are generally three feet deep with a seating ledge.

Our potting shed office has a far-infrared sauna that is forty-two inches wide. I love it after a long travel day or hard work in the garden.

Sometimes a sense of order
is preferred above the wild,
especially in the mountains
where rampant growth soon
consumes the hillsides. Kinsey
and Gordon Harper created
a tiny formal garden that
provides a veiled view to the
hillside below with espaliered
apple trees and a weathered
lattice by Country Casual.

CHAPTER 7

Gardening Is Therapy

124

Nurturing plants is fun! It's also a beneficial activity for any age group. The act of tending and weeding puts you into the arms of nature and the zone of responsibility. Enhanced flexibility, strength and self-esteem are common results of gardening. Immediate gratification at seeing a garden weeded or producing fruit does wonders for the mental condition of a stressed-out executive. Good nutrition is a bonus reward for tending vegetables.

If you are recovering from surgery, cancer treatment or in any way challenged physically, assistance from a horticultural therapist might be just the thing to help you in gardening for health. This exciting field is defined by the American Horticultural Therapy Association as the engagement of a person in gardening activities that are facilitated by a trained therapist. The field of horticultural therapy is rapidly growing as evidence-based design applications help patients regain strength and flexibility, reduce medication and regain a positive outlook on life as they recover from spinal, brain, bone and burn injuries, plus degenerative conditions caused by disease and aging. Used in this medical sense, horticultural therapy is useful to people of all abilities, ages and backgrounds. Specially educated and trained members of horticultural therapy rehabilitation teams work with doctors, occupational therapists and psychologists to bring improvement to the lives of their patients.

In the context of this book, the concept of horticultural therapy is used in a broader context. The act of creating and maintaining a place to garden on your property—be it kitchen, vegetable, or flower garden, wildflower meadow, a bonsai collection, or orchard or raiser flowerbeds—is considered to be a form of horticultural therapy, or gardening for health.

This broader definition of horticultural therapy encourages you to pursue self-directed treatment outdoors in nature. As you prune your shrubs, fertilize the garden and connect with the web of life, your lungs, heart, muscles and mind are exercised in both active and passive ways that enhance your well-being.

Lifelong Landscape
PATTERNS & PLACES

FRAGRANCE

Aromatherapy is an ancient form of alternative medicine. It uses volatile plant materials or essential oils, along with other aromatic compounds for therapeutic purposes. It is known to beneficially alter one's mind, mood, cognitive function and/or health.

Aromatherapy and scent can greatly increase the quality of sleep. Neuroscientists discovered that a rose scent substantially reduced sleep disturbances. Research shows that certain scents can soothe, invigorate and affect our moods and stress levels. Since the earliest of times, humans have used fragrances from nature for many purposes, including religious rituals, aphrodisiacs and to cover odors.

It is believed that the use of incense originated in ancient Egypt. Mostly used in religious ceremonies, gum resin and oleo gum resin of aromatic trees were imported from the Arabian and Somal coasts. Remnants of these perfumes have been found in archeological digs or through ancient texts. The formula for incense has hardly changed today: it is composed of aromatic plant materials and is often combined with essential oils. Aromatherapy does not cure conditions but helps the body to find a natural way to cure itself and improve immune response.

LEFT AND LOWER:
Sharon Daggett's beautiful conservatory in Spokane, Washington, is a haven during a hectic life and a sunny respite in the winter.

Conservatory

CONSERVATORIES AND GREENHOUSES

Sharon Daggett's conservatory garden in Spokane, Washington, is fully utilized year round. Whether it is in hosting a wedding, sharing tea with a friend or gardening to produce flowers on a dreary winter day, Sharon finds 100 percent satisfaction in her conservatory. Sizes of conservatories and greenhouses vary from a small hobbyist greenhouse that is 8 x 12 feet to double and triple the size. Sharon's greenhouse is special in that it includes cold frames that face the house, therefore extending the season of vegetable cultivation.

Parsley

Sage

Rosemary

Oregano

Thyme

Herb Garden

ABOVE: A mix of kale and myositis complement the vegetable garden at the Chicago Botanic Garden.

RIGHT: The Valenta guest-parking slot is adjacent to this special little kitchen garden. The rosemary in the tree trunk hides the propane source to the tower below. Dustin Watson of Scotty's Yard installed the entire property.

HERB GARDEN

Herb Gardens are places generally of small scale and contain a plant palette of fragrant, culinary or medicinal plants. Herb gardens are unique in garden history as they migrated in the twentieth century from kitchen gardens into a separate garden space.

I love herb gardens. In many ways, they are the classic repositories of garden lore, for each plant has a cultivated history. Plants are myriad and can include specialized chocolate mint, a calendula for dyeing cotton or wool, an Echinacea for medicinal use or ladies bedstraw to cleanse visitor's sheet.

These gardens are romantic; they offer us a slice of domestic purposefulness that is as integral to our evolution as humans as the wheel.

Inspiration: A rising sun bravely awakens a misty morning with a ray behind the shadow of a sundial. A soft fragrance of basil mixes with lavender as droplets of water roll off edges of mature leaves. The pattern garden, with cutwork beds for a minimum of plans, slowly comes into view. An edging line of parsley outlines the raised-brick beds and a frill of a mother of thyme inches its way toward the stone infill in the path.

BELOW AND RIGHT:
Gardening in the country provides challenges and opportunities. At Blackberry Farm's Toad Hall, Kreis Beall arranged mature apple trees into a formal orchard and enclosed her kitchen garden with espaliered Granny Smiths for easy pickins!

Best looking: Use a mixed medley of brick, wood or stone edging beds set into small bits of expanded slate inset with a mix of thyme and mint.

ORCHARD/FRUIT TREES

An orchard is an iconographic symbol of man's relationship to nature. Whether in a pasture, a garden, a front yard or an urban area, it stands alone. We feel connected to an orchard, especially ancient orchards with the neat rows and friendly domed shapes. Orchards are intimately connected to the web of life, and, as such, need water, good soil, decent weather and pollinators. How many trees constitute an orchard—two or twenty-two? An orchard can be mixed with apples and pears and welcome a fringe of figs on the perimeter. Lemons and orange trees mix well. It is all about similar requirements and pruning.

The French Kitchen Garden of Louis VIII at Versailles has an amazing museum of ancient fruit tree espaliers, orchard fruit examples and the live product. Sketches illustrate the deft manner of pruning to create narrow, tailored trees, especially useful in small areas.

BELOW: Magnificent fountains were part gardening therapy and part glamour in European estates. In America, this lovely ensemble at the home of David and Kristin Griffin in Oklahoma City, Oklahoma, blends tradition with multitasking. The top level offers a quiet respite from the child's play in the adjacent swimming pool and great lawn.

RIGHT: In Sea Island, Georgia, this courtyard fountain provides countless hours of quiet background sound. Frogs love the lily pads and the 30/70 ratio of vegetation reduces algal boom. The heron is Italian and chosen by Wendy and Tom Dowden.

Espaliered trees need about thirty-six inches in a row and a three-tiered apple or pear stands about sixty inches tall. Often, long grass is left around trees and a simple path is mowed once a month. An orchard eventually has to stop. Plant the adjacent woodland with blueberries or soft fruit berries at the edge for transition.

In Europe and Asia, where land is a premium, planting fruit trees on common land between buildings is very beneficial. Fruit trees humanize public spaces by being good providers. A fruit tree gives and asks no questions. The growth of cities seems to destroy these trees and the qualities they possess. Encourage small orchards to be planted in common land; community groups can care for the trees and harvest the fruit. Orchards often encourage a feeling of mutual benefit and responsibility. This naturally involves people taking care of them, thus they can be more beneficial than flowering trees in a community.

ORNAMENTAL FOUNTAIN

The ornamental fountain has a rich and long history. In early Pompeian gardens, archaeology revealed the lavish extent of ornamental fountains within dwellings. Fountains were considered a

necessity for the enjoyment of life and even figured on the frescoed walls.

For stand-alones, decisions relate to height of the basin for an eighteen-inch seating wall, one of my favorite combinations, or having it flush with grade. What materials should be used for coping, walls and the interior? Take your cues from the house and echo its construction.

If your fountain calls for greenery, remember the golden rule: 70 percent water surface coverage above or below the surface. If the fountain has a feature, use plants with a diversity of heights to frame the feature.

POTTING SHED

A potting shed is an integral part to any avid gardener's yard. Whether it is for practical purposes or to add character to your garden, sheds are great for storing tools, bags of dirt, supplies, wheelbarrows and the like. My green-roofed potting shed houses far more than tools; it is also a place for canning, herbal storage, my computer and a sauna. This multipurpose outdoor workshop is sized 20 x 24 feet and has a spacious twelve-foot-deep porch.

BELOW: Gardening as therapy means many things including the healthy cultivation of food for the table in all its forms. Soft fruits are some of my favorites. Berries are low, slow carbohydrates beneficial for weight loss.

RIGHT AND FACING: Raised beds, such as these at the Chicago Botanic Garden demonstrate how to garden at different levels to allow wheelchair access for cultivation for herbs, flowers and vegetables.

Soft Fruit

SOFT FRUIT

By soft fruit, I mean strawberries, blackberries, loganberries, raspberries and blueberries. It is amazing how much space these sprawling crops take. The English have perfected the soft fruit enclosure. These large mesh cages keep larger birds out and repel raccoons and smaller varmints completely. Our friends, Gillian and Paul from Bath, England, have a very clever kitchen garden with a compartment for soft fruits. They carefully net the plants during the fruiting season and

enjoy large, ripe raspberries in season. The rows are really quite short, perhaps twelve feet long and hold about four plants.

Chicken wire is a useful cladding, as soft fruits need lots of sun and water. With judicious pruning, soft fruits are easily managed when tied to a central row of support canes. For cultivation and maintenance, build a thirty-six-inch frame of large squares of wire and wood posts on which to tie the wild canes. Mow between rows, and prune ungainly canes as needed.

Soft fruit grown by friend Pat Hartrampf are somehow immune to marauding birds and beasts. Her field of 'Lady in Red' raspberries is a delight to walk among, picking lots of plump, juicy drupes.

RAISED FLOWERBEDS

A raised bed is so much easier to garden in than one flat on the ground. If you are gardening for health, consider a bed to at least eighteen inches tall and no more than five feet wide.

TOPIARY

A topiary is a plant that is trained to develop a clearly defined shape, often geometric or fanciful. Most topiary are woody evergreen shrubs with small leaves or needles, allowing the production of dense foliage. Whether used as hedges or columnar shapes to frame entryways or thresholds, topiaries add a bit of whimsy to a garden.

Lifelong
Landscape
ACTIVITIES

BONSAI
Miniature trees and liliputian natural landscapes may sound difficult, but bonsai are really easy and gratifying and take very little room.

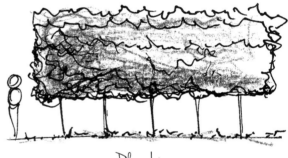

LEFT: The Asheville Arboretum in North Carolina is a candy box of ideas of how to grow exquisite bonsai. Some are placed in slabs of man-made terrain and some are on shelves of slate.

LOWER: The Chicago Botanic Garden has an amazing array of pleached, shaped and pruned trees that exhibit high horticultural art. In particular, this pleached allee of pears provides shade and acts as a connector to other garden rooms in the vegetable patch.

Pleaching

PLEACHING

Pleaching is the technique of training trees into a raised hedge (such as a palisade). Trees are planted in lines and then shaped to form a flat plane above ground level. Eventually, the tree's branches will begin to grow together and form a solid mass or wall-like structure.

BELOW: A French pot from La Madelaine is winter proof and presents a large vessel. The finish was distressed by the factory.

RIGHT: Choice of pots abound. At Highcote, we use whisky barrels to grow crops by rotation; one year it is tomatoes, then potatoes, then lettuces, plus copious amounts of compost.

POTS AND POTTED PLANTS

Gardens don't have to be large. A pretty specimen in a pot can bring a world of pleasure to a small balcony or terrace, or adorn a tight corner to accent architecture. The best part about pots is that they are easily changed and can hold seasonal plantings or miniature trees. Choose your pots with care, and if you have a collection, be

UPPER: Wisley in England is known for chic planting displays like this purple pot and complements perennials.

ABOVE: A tufa stone from Newfoundland provides positive drainage for a mixture of cold hardy sedums at Ushuata in North Carolina.

sure to group them together for impact and convenience of watering.

VEGETABLE GARDEN IN POTS

All gardens, both public and private, need a patch where vegetables can be grown. In a healthy town, every family can grow vegetables for themselves. It is a fundamental part of human life; vegetables are the only foods that are wholly able to support human life. They also help connect us to the land, which is something that parks, trees and manicured lawns cannot do.

Vegetable gardening in pots is a great way to contain edibles. Each pot can have a separate plant, such as a cherry tomato, with a skirt of parsley or arugula.

Lonesome Valley in
Cashiers, North Carolina,
is an oasis of sustainability
featuring community
garden, five-star dining
from garden to table, and
quality family activities
in a setting preserved in
perpetuity.

CHAPTER 8

The Healthy House & Living Communities

138   A healthy house can be hard to find. Drinking water quality, air free
of mold and mildew, thoughtfully organized room arrangements and
energy efficiency are deficient in most domestic structures. During
the baby boom of the nineteen fifties and sixties, suburban lots were
created that promoted neither energy conservation nor sound site-
planning principles.

Land use patterns today are evolving as sustainable, lifelong communities providing ease of public transportation, social networks,
community gardens and conservation of resources. An aging house
can be retrofitted to provide an ameliorative living environment,
but the larger picture of community needs is a much more complex
problem.

Charleston, South Carolina, is hot in the summer and relatively mild in the winter, thus sun pockets are greatly valued. Early-eighteenth-century dwellings often featured many windows and open doors for cross-ventilation.

Utopia +
Spirit of Place

Seeking utopia is a time-honored pursuit. What makes a community a lifelong neighborhood? Housing is affordable, located close to services, accessible and available within existing communities consisting of all age groups. Transportation offers motility choices to ensure aging individuals can access basic lifestyle needs. Healthy lifestyles include environments that promote physical activity, social interaction and easy access to health care facilities. Access to services and communication and educational needs are critical for long-term residents to be active and engaged. Community gardens and allotment plots round out the scenario.

Finding utopia is a process. It is both a place and a sense of place, a sense of fulfillment and the power of purpose. Whether it be in a lifelong planned community or a home you just purchased, utopia is a frame of mind within a physical surrounding.

Create a
Home Utopia

Who wouldn't want a home utopia, a place that seamlessly connects the mind of the land with the body of your house and creates a unique spirit of place? It is integrated, streamlined and functional from street to house to garden. Sensitive to its microcosm of nature, a utopia has a sustainable footprint. It has an unforgettable presence and is at peace with its four parts.

Land, the mind, is connected to nature through air, water, earth, wind and wood, and is thus called land-mind. House, the body, is connected to roads, electricity, utilities and civil services, and we call this house-body. The spirit of the place, the unique presence of your property, is released and experienced when the land-mind and house-body work in harmony.

How does this translate to the dwelling stages of man? Fresh from college, we live in apartments or small, shared houses. A balcony is the land-mind; a condominium complex is the house-body. Later, as a couple or family unit, the larger house-body rests on a more complex piece of land. With elders, the trend is to realize a smaller unit on a brilliantly integrated property.

Collaboration on this sanctuary combined our talents with Richard Skinner, AIA, of Jacksonville, to organize space around the new pool.

For a young career person to create a place with spirit, it may be a struggle, but what better time in life to initiate your own outdoor mind-body-spirit style? A very small oasis is well worth the effort. A fountain or wind chime, a compact place to dine outside, an aquarium and a couple of resilient plants are a great formula. Use color in pots and grow a smattering of herbs purchased from the grocery store. The demands of workplace and lack of ownership or funds coupled with desire to socialize result in creative solutions, but you can easily begin the process of learning how to knit together the parts. The process of feng shui, using a bagua, is a great beginning point since it helps orient you to the layout and connectivity within your home. Plus, it is fun!

Unleash the mind-body-spirit of your property. Whether purchasing your first home, moving a growing family into larger digs, changing neighborhoods or downsizing into a compact unit, your dwelling is an investment of dreams, time and money, and you want to get it right.

CREATE A SANCTUARY

The mind of the site and the body of a new house are seldom at peace. The design of your potential home sanctuary, with its unique spirit of place, is a time-honored process. Your dwelling, the body of the property, can work symbiotically with the mind of the land. The resultant spirit of place is the physical manifestation of a harmonious lifestyle. Because your property is as unique as a fingerprint, it has a particular set of environmental and functional concerns that are influenced by nature, housing shape and density.

HOUSE SITE

The hub, the body of the property, is the dwelling that is affected by and contributes to enjoyment of all the parts. A large, sprawling family home with multiple dependencies impacts the land—the mind of the property—far differently than a compact home with a small footprint and no dependencies.

Study your home on plan and in elevation using photographs and sketches, to see how to best integrate the horizontal and vertical design of the house and its grounds.

At Home
on the Range

JOHN ISCH, architect in Cincinnati, Ohio, was invited to brainstorm a home for an extended family in a dramatic country setting. The approach is over pretty countryside to view the house, which features comfortable rooflines and a warm expression. In siting the house, Isch took advantage of views both to the house as guests made their way across the pasture and from the house into the hills beyond. Perimeter spaces include multiple outdoor terraces to enjoy seasonal weather and al fresco meals. Destinations are limited as there are acres to explore!

BELOW: Architect Martin Shofner designed this elegant home in Nashville, Tennessee, to take advantage of a knoll.

RIGHT: This sunny courtyard in Louisiana presents a place for the grandparents to dine with their children. The stone benches are petrified wood that complement the green Chinese bluestone and cobblestone edging of tumbled crab orchard stone. Tulip magnolias, *Magnolia × soulangeana,* complete the scene. In five years, this courtyard will be well shaded with a canopy of leaves.

Landscape Patterns for Site Design

The observations of early Greek and Roman architects, repeated and adapted for hundreds of years, were improved and modified as man improved his living environments. Over time, a pattern language emerged, whereby the man's activities on the land could be diagrammed, generalized and best use surmised.

Christopher Alexander, in *A Pattern Language,* published in 1973, sought to define these time-honored systems. Of the hundreds of life patterns that Alexander identified, he only scratched the surface of landscape design. We used his work as a springboard for our own pattern language of landscape design.

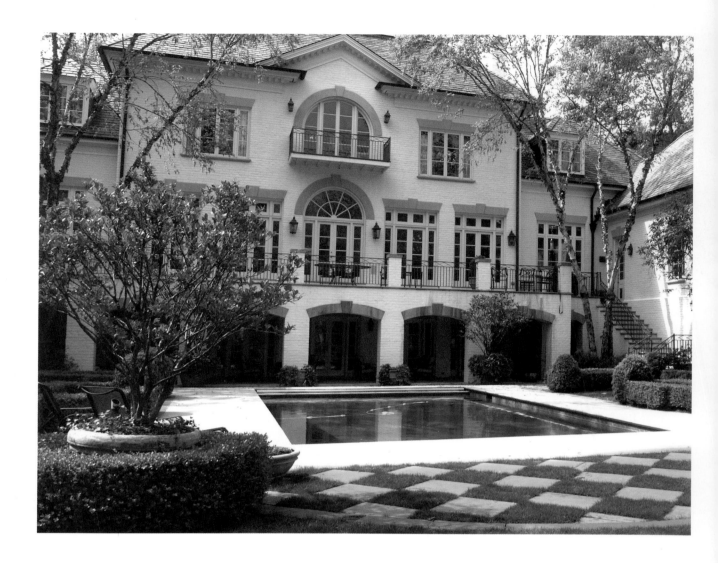

TYPICAL HOUSE PATTERNS AND SITE PLANS

So how is your property structured? Is it a townhouse with zero lot lines, a home in a grid of streets in a new neighborhood with a cul-de-sac, an estate or mountain cottage?

Today, it's common for a town home with a zero lot line to be set adjacent to another townhouse. A small courtyard is in the rear and a parking court in front. Designs on such a small canvas must multitask. Space planning is tight and the use of art elements and design principles paramount. There is only one chance to get it right because you see the whole enchilada all the time.

A step up in size and complexity is the typical grid pattern, nineteenth- and twentieth-century land plan that did not take into account Mother Nature's rivers, mountains, sun angles or shade trees. Sound like places you live in or have visited? Yes, this is typical of the great suburban sprawl.

ABOVE: In Atlanta, Georgia, this home designed by Barry Fox, AIA, provides a spacious courtyard for family entertainment surrounded by loggias and balconies.

FACING: Architect George Hopkins used sinker cypress throughout this Pearl River, Louisiana, home. The three brick terraces provide shady, private and public space.

House Organized

In considering how man dwells, *A Pattern Language* by Christopher Alexander kept cropping up in my library as documentary evidence of ideal relationships between man and his living environment. The following are useful guidelines.

INDOOR SUNLIGHT

Light in a dwelling is of utmost importance. Alexander suggests an "intimacy gradient" that marks rooms and areas along a space that needs the most sunlight. The theory of southern exposure is welcomed; important rooms are placed along the south edge of the building, while the building itself should be spread on an east-west axis.

POSITIVE OUTDOOR SPACE AND THE OUTDOOR ROOM

The courtyard is a positive outdoor space. Positive spaces are shaped by their enclosures and do not spill indefinitely into shapeless space. Per Alexander, "The shape of the outdoor space is just as important as the shape of the building that surrounds it."

USING A BAGUA

Creative ideas abound in site planning in order to merge the mind-body-spirit of your property. An interesting study is the use of the bagua, a planning overlay that orients your home to the most auspicious points for a happy and productive life. The bagua is divided into eight cardinal points of the compass, and each

BELOW AND FACING: This private garden in Charleston is a marvelous example of a near perfect golden rectangle. The front portion of the street side aligns with a gate screen off the body of the house and makes a rectangular garden. The rear pool garden occupies a square shape that divides neatly into paving for access to the formal garden and kitchen house, plus ample grass to entertain beside the rectangular pool. This area is approximately one-third grass, one-third brick paving and one-third pool and is very pleasing to the eye.

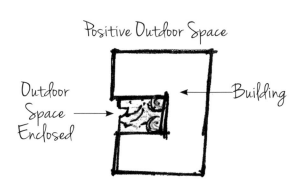

Positive Outdoor Space

Outdoor Space Enclosed → Building

point has a relationship name. When something is going odd in your life, you can affect cures on your home to remedy the problem. For instance, if you want to have easy money, position the wealth point across from your front door. This technique is usually done for house cures.

To begin, find north by using a compass. Refer to your survey and place a transparency of the bagua diagram over your site plan for general reference. With north found, a transparency of a bagua in hand and overlaid on a master plan on a raw piece of land, adding

a sunrise/sunset diagram, relating to canopy trees, with north identified and a sketch transferred to your property for a possible housing form, you are combining eastern and western site-planning skills to get the highest and best use out of your house.

THE GOLDEN RECTANGLE

Aesthetics and geometry often dictate site organization on paper. An interesting formula that we discovered while living in Charleston, designing courtyards in the strict confines of the historic district, was that when rectangular

A Gracious Courtyard

IN THE BUCKHEAD area of Atlanta, Georgia, gracious dwellings set in spacious grounds are the norm. However, not all of them have a design team who collaborate to think through every detail before beginning major work. The design brief for this home on Tuxedo Road included a request for at least two enclosed courtyards. The rear-facing west courtyard is enclosed by the wings of the house. "This configuration is what everyone wants," says architect Norman Askins. "It's the light and feeling you are looking into the garden as you walk around the house." The lot slopes dramatically from north to south, resulting in a tall retaining wall on the south side. This bonus feature provides a sheltered wall for a retreat from the hot Atlanta weather. There are plenty of shady benches and leisurely walkways to enjoy simply being outside.

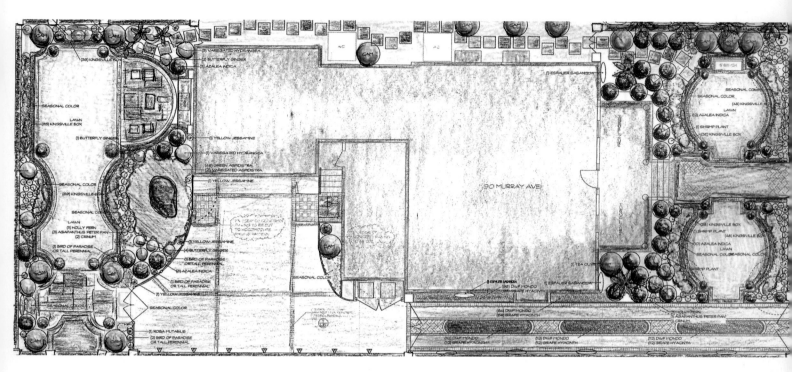

The various plant labels visible in the garden plan include: (36) KINGSVILLE, (3) VARIEGATED HYDRANGEA, (1) BUTTERFLY GINGER, (3) AZALEA INDICA, SEASONAL COLOR, LAWN, (89) KINGSVILLE BOX, (1) BUTTERFLY GINGER, (1) YELLOW JESSAMINE, (1) VARIEGATED HYDRANGEA, (48) GREEN ASPIDISTRA, (2) VARIEGATED ASPIDISTRA, (1) YELLOW JESSAMINE, SEASONAL COLOR, (69) KINGSVILLE BOX, SEASONAL COLOR, LAWN, (1) HOLLY FERN, (3) AGAPANTHUS PETER PAN, (2) CRINUM, (1) BIRD OF PARADISE OR TALL PERENNIAL, (1) YELLOW JESSAMINE, (4) BUTTERFLY GINGER, (1) BIRD OF PARADISE OR TALL PERENNIAL, (3) AZALEA INDICA, (3) BIRD OF PARADISE OR TALL PERENNIAL, (1) YELLOW JESSAMINE, SEASONAL COLOR, (1) ROSA MUTABILIS, (2) BIRD OF PARADISE OR TALL PERENNIAL, '90 MURRAY AVE', (1) ESPALIER SASANQUA, SEASONAL COLOR, LAWN, (12) AZALEA INDICA, (2) SHRIMP PLANT, (30) KINGSVILLE BOX, (38) KINGSVILLE BOX, (2) SHRIMP PLANT, (44) KINGSVILLE BOX, (10) AZALEA INDICA, LAWN, SEASONAL COLOR, SHRIMP PLANT, (1) TEA OLIVE, (8) BRAKE MANDA, (36) DWF MONDO, (36) GRAPE HYACINTH, (1) ESPALIER SASANQUA, (1) HOLLY FERN, (3) AGAPANTHUS PETER PAN, (1) CRINUM, (64) DWF MONDO, (64) GRAPE HYACINTH, (12) DWF MONDO, (12) GRAPE HYACINTH, (12) DWF MONDO, (12) GRAPE HYACINTH, (12) DWF MONDO, (12) GRAPE HYACINTH

lots predominate, the golden rectangle magically works to your advantage.

The golden ratio is 1:1.618, which results in a distinctive rectangular shape. When a square is removed, the remainder is another golden rectangle with the same proportions as the first.

SUNNY SOUTH SIDE OUT

For hundreds of years, designers and architects have agreed that sun is good for man and that outdoor spaces should face south. This makes buildings and gardens happy places. To reinforce this design theory, lots designed longer from north to south with houses placed on the north side of the lot encourage a south-facing exposure.

GARDENS ENCLOSED BUT VISIBLE

Fencing around sides and fronts of properties to enclose garden spaces helps shape the fundamental layout of homes. The presence of a large tree can influence the relative position of a building on its site. The theory of south

side, sunny side out can guide the placement of a private but visible garden. Front gardens are adjacent to the home and enclosed by a partial wall.

LIVING IN COURTYARDS

In order for a courtyard to be successful, it should meet four specific criteria: views out of it to a larger space, two or three doors open

FACING: A sunny front on Murray Boulevard is shaded by palmettos and live oaks. Liz and Doug MacIntyre love the balancing parterres and invite birds to frequent the garden at the feeder. The gate screen provides privacy from joggers along the waterfront.

Sunny Front Entry

IN CHARLESTON, South Carolina, a south-facing garden fronts the Murray Boulevard along the historic levee. The main living rooms are located at this end of the house as well as the front door. The garden takes advantage of this exposure by offering a balanced pair of grass rugs, perfect for viewing the nearby ocean from carefully placed benches.

Sustainability techniques also take advantage of the south face by providing grass lozenges in the driveway. The rear garden is loaded with shade-loving plants, an arbor and a fountain placed away from the strong winds experienced in the front of the house.

Our forefathers were no strangers to terracing to make the most of a steep slope. At the Governor's Palace in Colonial Williamsburg, terraces adjacent the kitchen house provide convenient vegetables for the table.

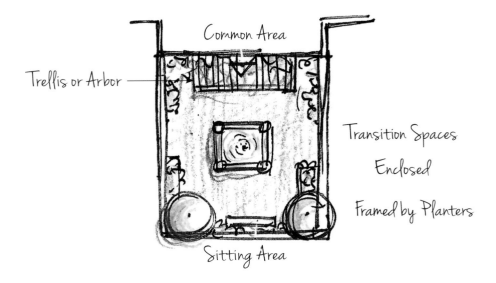

Trellis or Arbor

Common Area

Transition Spaces

Enclosed

Framed by Planters

Sitting Area

into it from a building, natural paths connect it from doors across the courtyard, and preferably it has a continuous roofed veranda or porch along one side.

Courtyards can fail. If one is too enclosed or does not have enough doors, it will become a fish bowl without animation. No one wants to be in a dead end or an airless space. Courtyards are aligned preferably along an east-west axis to keep in heat during the winter and heat out during the summer months. The benefit is that the interior home climate is easier to regulate.

CREATING TERRACES FOR USEFUL OUTDOOR SPACES

From mountains to the rolling hills of the countryside, terraces provide space for gardening, entertaining, playing and simply a vantage point to enjoy nature. To conceptualize terraces during the site-planning stage is very important. Decide on how much room is needed to, for example, park a set of cars, to provide for a dining table with room to walk around it, or for rock walls to hold up space for a potting shed.

Trees equal shade and habitat and a healthy earth. Preserve the trees on your site for posterity and plant more. This home blends sustainable paving choices around the pool to transition between nature and man.

UTILIZE TREES

In preparing a mind-body-spirit, analysis, the body of the house can tap into the resources of the mind of the land, its trees! Energy efficiency is achieved through planting shade trees on the west and southern portions of the property to cool the roof during the summer months. For wind control, plant evergreens on the northwest quadrant of your property. For winter sunlight, only plant deciduous trees on the south, sunny side of the house.

Lifelong
Landscape
Patterns
AND PLACES

GREEN ROOFS

A green roof is exactly how it sounds—a roof that is covered in plants, hence the word and color "green." They are great additions to any household trying to lessen its ecological footprint. Green roofs help lessen storm-water runoff as well as making overall neglected spaces useful. Green roofs are especially beneficial in large urban areas due to their ability to reduce the heat island effect, a condition in which city and suburban developments absorb and trap heat.

At the Cravey house in Cashiers, the entire landscape needed to be shoehorned into a steep hillside. By carefully shaping the spaces, a circular route was created around the property and tall walls became hanging gardens.

CHAPTER 9

The Master Plan

A seamless, lifelong living environment is at your fingertips! In beginning a plan, take into consideration the eight principle landscape patterns as well as the inherent four parts of the landscape: the approach and arrival, the hub, perimeter, and destinations. The process of designing your utopian property is a continuous work in progress—Mother Nature, you and your goals. No two properties are quite alike; the environment and use patterns differ across the board. A site map that explores relationships will infuse your property with lifelong landscape patterns.

Lifelong landscape design assesses the raw, built and living landscape. Art elements and design principles, plus time-honored site-planning techniques, such as feng shui and traditional overlays, provide a structure to create functional and aesthetic environments. Few of us understand the mature size of trees and shrubs and want to design a garden that multitasks with environmental solar and wind control. Tree places, such as the pair, avenue, grove, square, espalier, hedge and green wall, are important personalities in a lifelong landscape design.

The Organized
Property

When Hugh and I were young in our design training, we spent every summer combing historic landscapes in America and abroad to see what made them tick. Was there a language of the land that was unique to each property? Were there tips we could glean about how forefathers lived that would make living on our land more integrated? What concepts might we use to improve our design philosophy that would make it timeless?

It didn't take long to uncover the mystery. Each property we studied was clearly divided into four inalienable parts. This is not rocket science, but we did take thoughtful analysis of many properties before it became clear. The approach and arrival sequence, hub, perimeter, and pathways and destinations are universal patterns of how man lives on the land. Each part is customizable to the site and layout of your unique property. This is the topic of *Timeless Landscape Design: The Four-Part Master Plan*, and it bears repeating major points here. This system makes it easy to focus on one area at a time, yet keeps the big picture always in mind.

THE APPROACH AND ARRIVAL SEQUENCE

In a nutshell, the approach and arrival sequence is the welcome mat you put out for visitors. It announces who you are and how you live. This part of the landscape includes the driveway, parking, front walk and entry gardens.

As a rule of thumb, make the landing at the front door at least eight feet deep and eight feet wide. The walkway in the front should be a comfortable five feet wide and meander in a purposeful way towards its destination, the front door. It

may lead to stairs and have room for visitors to put down umbrellas or gifts on a spacious landing before being greeted.

Parking areas must be obscured so that the arrival sequence sets up the house as a distinguished entity, a strong presence. Cars are too prosaic to be part of the immediate sequence. Give yourself some space to park at least twenty feet away from the front door, if at all possible. If not, in a close townhome environment, a five-foot buffer of hedged greenery will suffice as a green wall to separate to the parking area.

FACING: In Sea Island, the material at the arrival sequence honors the architecture in color and texture.

ABOVE: This mountain landscape uses vernacular materials. The drive apron is a welcome mat of large stones.

BELOW AND FACING:
This pool in the perimeter
of the Feebe courtyard
in New Orleans is close
to the house and well
located for both exercise
and entertainment.

are linkages, or walkways. Here, the journey is as important as the destination. Accessibility is key. Think of destinations as being pearls on a necklace that winds around, and ultimately returns, to its point of beginning after a nice stroll.

The litany of places to include as destinations on your property is vast. A kitchen garden, cutting garden, herb garden pleasure ponds, stroll gardens, places for a dog, compost garden, a retreat, swimming pool, active play areas, passive outdoor seating areas—the world is your oyster. Each place requires a set amount of space and planning to get the most of your limited outdoor space.

The approach and arrival sequence, hub, perimeter, and pathways and destinations are universal patterns of how man lives on the land. Because each part is customizable to the site and layout of your unique property, one never really quite gets it all finished. But once it is, it is timeless and at peace.

Checklist for Destinations

WHAT DO YOU like to do? Or better yet, what would you like to do outside if given no parameters other than the size and orientation of your property? The best thing about a four-part master plan is that you can draw and dream to your heart's content, well before the contractor arrives to plant the first tree or pour footings for a project.

• A vegetable garden requires a minimum of a 40 x 40-foot space to provide a diversity of foods, a compost area to make the most of recycled green goods, and water for irrigation.

• A destination retreat may be 8 x 12 feet for a small covered structure.

• Active recreation facilities such as swimming pools require a professional to install and call upon the best professionals for advice. It is worth every penny.

• Destinations require pathways or visual indicators for wayfinding. Plan maintenance into your destination sequence by providing walkways at five feet wide to allow for plant growth and lawn mower access.

• Landscape patterns such as the circular walk are stress reducers. Visit www.dargan.com/landscapeyourlife/bonuslandscape_patterns for more than 200 different landscape patterns. A bonus for readers is included.

Design a
Master Plan

You don't have to be a rocket scientist to draw creative solutions for the perfect lifelong landscape. Not many of us have studied landscape or environmental design, much less know how to make a property functional without the aid of an expert. Welcome to the tricks of the trade. In this section, you will be able to assess the potentials of your existing, or raw, landscape, challenge yourself to seek sustainable solutions with building materials, and maximize the structural and horticultural use of plants in your home environment.

Drawing your own special environment is simple using raw, built and living landscape

This raw landscape on Montagu Street in Charleston, South Carolina, features a list of wishes and desires that includes screening the neighboring view to creating a revitalized courtyard. In creating a base sheet, plotting the existing trees is crucial in decision-making. Here, the owner is testing the height of hedging needed to shield the neighboring view.

concepts. This creative, integrative method provides tools to both assess and maximize the potential of your home landscape.

The organized property, something we each desire to simplify and accommodate to our changing lifestyles, is based on the genetic code of your domicile. As discussed in the previous section, each place has a unique four-part master plan of approach and arrival sequence, hub, perimeter, and pathways and destinations.

The needs analysis is the dream sequence a homeowner may enjoy as he peers into the foreseeable future. Is this home temporary for one, two or three years? Is it a place to raise children through school? Or is the homeowner planning to retire on this piece of land? Many of these considerations were discussed in chapter two to help you focus on the program best suited to your long- or short-term enjoyment.

Another method for organizing thoughts is to simply draw ideas on photographs. Put your photographs into a gallery and print them four or six to a sheet. Then let your imagination run wild as you sketch solutions to hide horrid views to a neighbor's garage or create an entry point to a garden. The small-scale photographs help you see the forest for the trees and not get too caught up in details. Then transfer these spatial ideas from the photograph to the plan to scale and, voila, you've integrated horizontal and vertical design.

A Highlands Courtyard

Be a spatial problem solver. Needs and design work hand in hand, especially when testing a site to recognize its potentials. The design process for this courtyard at the Highlands Country Club in Highlands, North Carolina, was to determine what functions could occur in the space, such as seating a small terrace for outdoor dining.

Sketches using art elements of line, form, color and texture plus the design principle of

focalization and balance came into play over photographs. The views into the courtyard now focus on the large bench. Softening ground covers between the cracks of the stones result in a relaxing solution to a front garden. Guests happily wait here and admire local perennials and hydrangeas in full bloom while the attendant brings the car.

FACING AND ABOVE: Before and after photos make the design process at Highlands Country Club seem easy. It went from a wasteland at the front door to a treasured seating area to visit with friends due to careful study during the design process.

ABOVE: The landing at the Gilbert home in Rome, Georgia, was a critical component to the pathway.

RIGHT: Here, the English steps are under construction at Ushuata in western North Carolina.

The Built Landscape

The *built landscape* features everything that involves construction of hardscapes for driveways and terraces, structures, utilities, water harvesting and specialty areas such as composting. Mastering the principles of sustainable design is informative; it opens the door to lifelong improvements on your property.

In setting up your sheet, think of a layer cake. Build upon the information from the earlier studies of needs analysis, site analysis and functionality of the existing landscape. It is not possible to show everything on the same sheet, so do overlays using transparent tissue paper on top of our base sheet of survey features.

Considerations of sustainable hardscapes, covered in chapter one, are useful as a springboard for final decisions. Sustainable techniques for functional hardscapes encourage drainage patterns between and around stones while using as little paving as possible. Remember, "form follows function," so place paving only where functionally needed. Often design for frugal hardscape uses natural materials, so investigate what is locally available.

Revisit the eight lifelong landscape design tenants and work them into your design. Connect

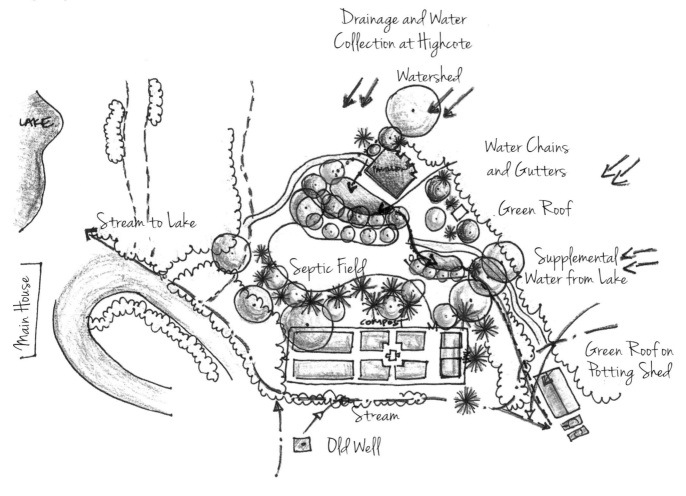

*Drainage and Water
Collection at Highcote*

Watershed

*Water Chains
and Gutters*

Green Roof

*Supplemental
Water from Lake*

Stream to Lake

Main House

Septic Field

*Green Roof on
Potting Shed*

Stream

Old Well

with the web of life, encourage social interaction with family and friends, offer places for active recreation, provide passive retreats, enhance choices for freedom of access, promote evidence-based stress reducers, and include horticultural therapy, such as growing vegetables or herbs. Employ a master plan working seamlessly towards these goals by integrating the four parts inherent of any landscape: the approach and arrival sequence, hub, perimeter and destinations with linkages.

SITE PROCESSES OF UTILITIES, WATER HARVESTING & COMPOSTING

Water harvesting and composting are essential kit in a lifelong landscape design. So add these components when mapping and analyzing complex site processes of drainage, vehicular movement, utilities and tree canopy on your property.

Rain gardens and water-harvesting designs employ knowledge of basic site processes to collect and disperse water. Water harvesting collects water for future use; rain gardens collect and disperse into the environment. Homeowners employ rain gardens, landscaped areas planted to wild flowers and other native vegetation that soak up rain water, mainly from the roof of a house, a drive or other building.

A typical residential rain garden ranges from 100 to 300 square feet. Rain gardens can be smaller than 100 square feet, but the smaller the garden, the less the plant variety. They are typically

This rain garden at the Platinum LEED–certified Chicago Botanic Gardens is as much an art form as a functional swale.

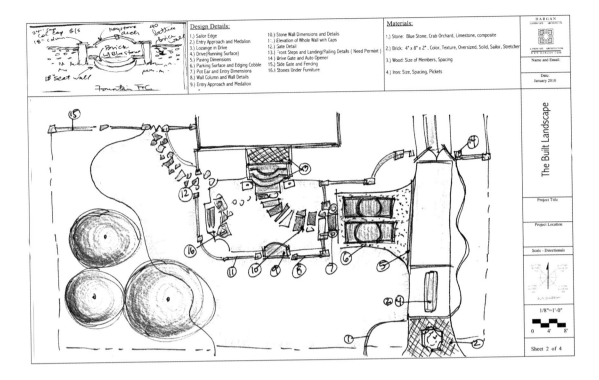

between four and eight inches deep. The rain garden fills with a few inches of water after a storm and the water slowly filters into the ground rather than running off to a storm drain. Compared to a conventional patch of lawn, a rain garden allows about 30 percent more water to soak into the ground. By reducing storm-water runoff, rain gardens can be a valuable part of storm-water control on a wider canvas. While an individual rain garden may seem like a small thing, collectively they produce substantial neighborhood and community environmental benefits.

Water-harvesting systems are important resources. To determine the amount of water available for collection, the square footage of the roofs of sheds, main house and garage is calculated. Charts are available to calculate how much rain is typically produced in a minute during a storm and this number is calculated to get the fluid gallons. Tanks, which range in size from small gutter barrels to large 20 x 5 x 4-foot 1,750-gallon behemoths to flexible, large plastic bladders that can be inserted in a home crawl space. Next comes the hard part, determining the water-consumption needs for your garden. An irrigation expert can provide gallons-per-minute information on the heads to deploy water. Multiply this by the amount recommended times the number of heads per zone times the number of zones, and you have a good idea of how much water it takes each time you irrigate. Most systems run two or three times a week, so figure for this and then determine how many weeks you want to water the garden from your cistern. It is not uncommon to need 20,000 gallons.

Placing the cistern is another process. In order for a backhoe to dig the holes, a retaining wall may need constructing to provide level ground, and the actual space for the cistern collection unit needs to be carefully planned and adjacent tree roots protected from compaction. Often, cisterns are placed under drives in least-used areas where the large manhole access covers can be accessed. These are not attractive, so an artificial turf rug or sedum ground cover is useful. The pump electricity varies with the size of your system, so an expert in plumbing and irrigation is recommended to size this equipment. Gutters need professional piping into the collection filter.

The benefit of having an automatic irrigation system that runs from cistern water is enormous. Many communities have limited water supply, and in times of drought, your irrigation system is restricted or terminated altogether. We had seventeen weeks of complete drought one spring that was impossible to believe in the mountains of a temperate rainforest. This occurrence made me a great believer in cisterns and water harvesting. Be prepared.

In Charleston, South Carolina, courtyard gardens multitask for many age groups and activities. An excellent example is The Benjamin Philips House Garden on Church Street, where places to dine reside in clearly defined garden rooms, or formal gardens set a stage for plant collections.

CHAPTER 10

Designs for the Stages of Life

Connecting with nature is the launching pad for lifelong landscape design principles. As man progresses through life, it is easy to overlook the benefit of being in nature due to the pressures of job, community needs and family life. Lifelong landscape design gives you a language of landscape patterns to intentionally bring nature back into your life.

Recent studies of places where the world's most happy and long-lived people reside offer insight into important lifestyle elements. Known as blue zones, where people commonly live active lives past the age of 100 years, five such places on Earth share lifelong lessons in connecting with nature while enjoying a healthy life. Elders living in Sardinia, Italy, Okinawa in Japan, Loma Linda in California, Nicoya Peninsula in Costa Rica, and Icaria in Greece have lifestyles worth studying. The lessons learned include eating a plant-based diet with more legumes, the importance of family, regular moderate activity, being socially active community members, financial security and living a purposeful life.

Taking a clue from the blue zone research, the emerging field of therapeutic landscape design documents the effects of nature and gardens on man's health and well-being. Using evidence-based design principles, therapeutic landscapes can reduce dependence on pain medicine, lower blood pressure, and reduce cortisol levels and stress on the mental and physical body. Hospitals are not necessarily mentally and physically conducive places to heal. Thoughtfully designed healing

gardens bring nature back into play as a powerful force. These techniques, coupled with lifestyle modification, form the basis for lifelong landscape designs.

Today, people have many choices of where to live, how to organize a household and what is required to live a happy and healthy life. Learning about nature and designing a lifelong landscape is cumulative. The average age of a first-time homeowner is thirty-three and the average move-up age is forty-five. Statistics show that an average person moves twelve to sixteen times in a lifetime, and stays in a home between five and seven years. The average size of a household is three persons. Given the probability of moving and a growing family, opportunities abound to tune up your outdoor design skills as you tackle the next home.

Domestic Dwellers

Designers of domestic landscapes identify four major groups of dwellers: children, a one- or two-person household, intergenerational families, and elders. Each group benefits from sensitive site design offering places that connect with the web of life, social interaction, active and passive recreation, are accessed easily by all levels of motility, and embrace evidence-based stress reducers and horticultural therapies. In addition, a healthy house is essential to the lifelong formula.

Children often prefer a natural landscape with boundaries and rough edges for creative play rather than a play structure. Single people or couples often dwell in homes with an outdoor dining area, a balcony or small garden, and a quiet place to relax. This group may choose a condominium or apartment in an urban area,

or a compact single-family home in a neighborhood with convenient transportation to shopping and work. Statistics show that residency changes more often with this group, so developing a lifestyle that promotes healthy living with streamlined landscape design is prudent.

The family with intergenerational user groups has, by necessity, a larger dwelling with flexible outdoor space. Popular venues include play areas designed to encourage exercise and connection with nature, places to entertain family and friends, a large vegetable garden,

ABOVE: In the historic Druid Hills area of Atlanta, Georgia, deep lots laid out by the Olmstead firm provide opportunities for compartmentalization of space. The spacious great lawn provides a place for soccer practice or a tented family party.

LEFT: Deerfield, an Episcopal retirement village in Asheville, North Carolina, provides spacious balconies, community vegetable gardens, pools, croquet to encourage social interaction and a healthy elder environment. My mother, Shirley Kelley Boone, admires a potted plant on her balcony.

Grandparents with limited mobility need convenient places to sit and watch children play and ramped access with limited grade changes.

A combination of hard and soft surfaces meets most needs for bike riding or climbing. Natural flat areas or ones created by decking or terracing are essential for successful play areas. The size can vary from a space 8 x 8 feet to a large baseball field or a 20 x 20-foot space for a play set.

Involve your child with the design of the garden and list all the items they like, determine the space needed, and know how much space you have available. Children benefit from both small and large areas in which to interact and develop active life skills.

Even an apartment complex can offer quality outdoor experience with a little effort. The best environments provide interpretive play areas designed to encourage connection with nature plus include observation and connection with their families. Learning how plants taste, feel, smell, sound and look reduces nature deficit syndrome.

Bond and Burke Almand practice skills on the great lawn. Lawn games encourage teamwork, balance, agility and endurance.

TIPS ON ENVIRONMENTS FOR FAMILIES

Nature: Natural play areas where children can create their own world enhances leadership skills and encourages them to be future stewards of the Earth, all while discovering that nature is a friendly place.

Freedom and Mobility: Watch for topographic changes; children love to walk on walls! Provide cushioned surfaces adjacent to play structures and install smooth running surfaces for bicycles and strollers.

Therapeutic: Activities in nature that allow direct contact with nature are evidence-based to produce similar hormones to certain medications used for attention deficit disorder. Touching plants helps reduce pain medications. Growing a garden allows children to connect with the web of life.

Social: Play areas—closely connected to the house with viewing areas set aside with benches for parents and caregivers—promote use of active and passive play, enhance social interaction and connectivity.

Active Use: A circular network of spaces linked by stroller or bicycle path can work in a space as small as twenty feet in diameter. A customized play set involves a space 8 x 8 feet or larger. A swimming pool occupies a much larger footprint of 12 x 35 feet or much more for water sports.

Passive Use: A place outside to read in the shade, practice writing skills, sing or rehearse on musical instruments fosters leadership and reinforces skillsets in an invigorating environment.

You may be surprised by the list of diverse uses your family needs and expects from household outdoor spaces. Involve your children, teenagers, elder parents and the caregivers in defining and creating the perfect environment. Keep an open mind and let the budget work in phases in order to obtain the highest and best use from the site. Well-planned outdoor spaces with timeless features in proportion to human occupation hold their value.

BELOW: Bocce ball is a popular activity at the Chattooga Club situated in a grove of ancient apple trees in Cashiers, North Carolina.

RIGHT: Teri Bond takes a breather from gardening in Highlands, North Carolina. Her pet Jack Russells, Thelma and Ralph, are invaluable garden companions. Teri's garden in the fall is a mix of old-fashioned perennials, left to seed for birds to eat over the winter.

Designing for Elders

Elders seek freedom to be safely and conveniently outside and unrestricted in their mobility with connection to nature. Retirement migration is a large factor in lifelong landscape design. For once, people have a chance to choose their environment in which to age in place, if they have not already. (see chapter three: Utopias). When it comes to elder

lifestyle, design for a more mental and spiritual side of life. Elders generally need far less land than most user groups.

Natural flat areas or ones created by decking or terracing are essential. The size can vary from a space 8 x 8 feet closely connected to the house with viewing areas slightly set aside with benches for family and caregivers. A circular network of spaces linked to paths can work in a space as small as twenty feet in diameter.

Involve your family and caregivers, spouse and therapist with the design of the garden and list all the items they suggest. Limited mobility requires convenient places to sit and watch children play. Provide ramped access and limited grade changes.

Conclusion

Ready to Design a Utopia?

The landscape patterns and activities of our home environments shape us as much as we shape them. Your home landscape is an evolution of personal experiences from every stage of life: child, adult or elder. As you accumulate a personal language of landscape preferences, these skills enhance the quality of your life. Whether you experiment with creating a balcony vegetable garden or a quiet retreat to de-stress from the day's activities, you are employing archetypal patterns of how man interacts with the landscape. The way he moves through it, and things he needs to be comfortable, safe and nourished are vast.

The multitude of landscape patterns for use, delight and health can be daunting. By envisioning your current outside environment as a stepping-stone to a lifelong landscape utopia, hold the ideals of healthy living close to your heart:

* Connect with the web of life
* Encourage social interaction with family and friends
* Offer places for active recreation and play
* Provide passive retreats
* Enhance choices for freedom and access
* Promote evidence-based stress reducers
* Include gardening for health as you tend your wares, your mind and body
* Complement a healthy house with clean air, water and an organized interior plan
* Employ a master plan working seamlessly towards these goals by integrating the four parts inherent of any landscape—the approach and arrival sequence, hub, perimeter and destinations with linkages, plus art elements, design principles and time-honored site-planning techniques

With these ideals ever present, you will be thinking about more than your garden. The next step involves encouraging neighborhoods to become lifelong communities that share home-grown produce, recycle, water harvest, compost and are watchful of each other's well-being.

Your utopia is at your fingertips.

Resources

Architects, Landscape Architects, Builders and Landscape Contractors

Norman Askins, Architect
normanaskins.com

Gerrie Bremmerman, Interior Designer
bremermanndesigns.com/
store/furniture_search.
php?RID=ImmWaGhpmpSY

Dargan Landscape Architects
dargan.com

Jack Davis, Architect
jackdavisarchitect.com

Bob Dews, Xstreme Landscapes and Ponds
xstreamponds.com

Barry Fox, Architect
barryfox.com

Myer, Greeson, Paullin and Benson
mgpb.com

Francie Hargrove Interiors
franciehargrove.com

Hickory Construction, Builder
hickoryconstruction.com

George Hopkins, Architect
georgehopkins.com

John Isch, Architect
rwaarchitects.com/en/
index.php?page=team

Al Platt, Architect
plattarchitecture.com

Louisa Pringle Cameron, Photographer
Martin Shofner, Architect
architectsure.com

Richard Skinner, Architect
rs-architects.com

Daryl Stewart, Builder

John Warren, Natural Landscapes
1992 Whiteside Cove Road
Highlands, NC 28741

Marcia Weber, Gardens to Love, and Mark Fleming
photo credit pp. 52, 71
gardenstolove.com

Appliances for the Garden

Chipper
Patriot Products CSV 3100B
amazon.com/Patriot-Products-CSV-
3100B-Stratton-Gas-Powered/
dp/B002KHVKQY/ref=sr_1_10?s=
lawn-garden&ie=UTF8&qid=
1337268811&sr=1-10

Compost Bins
Bokashi Indoor Composter
amazon.com/SCD-Probiotics-
K101-Seasons-Composter/dp/
B004X5KB0W/ref=sr_1_5?ie=
UTF8&qid=1337268276&sr=8-5

Compost Tea Maker
Growing Systems
Compost Tea Maker
amazon.com/dp/B003B0YCY6?
tag=compostsoup-20&link_code=
as3&creative=373489&camp=211189

Compost Tumbler
Envirocycle Composter
envirocycle.com

Vermiculture Systems
Worm Factory
amazon.com/Worm-Factory-
DS3GT-3-Tray-Composter/dp/
B000S6LZBO/ref=sr_1_1?ie=
UTF8&qid=1337268733&sr=8-1

Specialty Products: Sculpture, Stone, Furniture

Brattleworks
brattleworks.com

Chattooga Gardens
chattoogagardens.com

Country Casual
countrycasual.com

Kenneth Lynch and Sons
klynchandsons.com

Lee Valley Tools
leevalley.com

Robinson Flagstone
robinsonflagstone.com

Dustin and Erin Watson, Scotlyn's Yard
141 Little Terrapin Road
Cashiers, North Carolina 28717
scotlandyardsgreenhouse.com

Lighting

The Outdoor Lights
photo credit pp. 31, 102–3
theoutdoorlights.com

Public Gardens

Chicago Botanic Garden
chicagobotanic.org

Colonial Williamsburg
colonialwilliamsburg.com

Heale House, England
healegarden.co.uk

Joyce Kilmer Memorial Forest
main.nc.us/graham/
hiking/joycekil.html

Len Foot Hike Inn
hike-inn.com

Pashley House, England
pashleymanorgardens.com

RHS Garden Wisley, England
rhs.org.uk/gardens/wisley

Private Country Club Gardens and Spas

Blackberry Farm
Wayland, Tennessee
blackberryfarm.com

Canyon Ranch
Tuscon, Miami and the Berkshires
canyonranch.com

Chattooga Club
Cashiers, North Carolina
chattoogaclub.com

The Cloister
Sea Island Georgia
seaisland.com

Deerfield, Ashevillle, North Carolina
deerfieldwnc.org

High Hampton Inn and Country Club
Cashiers, North Carolina
highhamptoninn.com

Highlands Country Club
Highlands, North Carolina
highlandscountryclub.com/
viewCustomPage.aspx?id=1

Hippocrates Health Institute
West Palm Beach, Florida
hippocratesinst.org

Lonesome Valley
Cashiers, North Carolina
lonesomevalley.com

Phantom Forest
Knisra, South Africa
phantomforest.com

Round Hill
Cashiers, North Carolina

Spring Forest
Cashiers, North Carolina

Wade Hampton
Cashiers, North Carolina
wadehamptongc.com

The Wortham House B&B
Charleston, South Carolina
vrbo.com/348976

Bibliography

Architectural Theory

Alexander, Christopher, Sara Ishikawa, and Murray Silverstein. *A Pattern Language: Towns, Buildings, Construction.* New York: Oxford University Press, 1977.

Pollan, Michael. *A Home of One's Own: The Architecture of Daydreams.* New York: Penguin Books, 1997.

Vitruvius. Ten Books on *Architecture* by *Vitruvius* (De Architectura – 15BCE). Translated by Morris Hicky Morgan, Ph.D, LL.D. Flemington, NJ: Agathon, 2007.

Eastern Landscape Philosophy

Baynes, Cary F., trans., *The I Ching or Book of Changes.* 2nd ed. Washington, D.C.: Bollinger Foundation, Inc., 1967.

Western Landscape Philosophy

Pope, Alexander. *Epistle to Burlington: The Vitruvian Analogies. Studies in English Literature, 1500–1900.* Houston: Rice University Press, 2005.

Thoreau, Henry David. *Walden, or Life in the Woods and, on the Duty of Civil Disobedience.* Signet, 1960.

Landscape Architecture and Planning

Arendt, Randall. *Growing Greener: Putting Conservation into Local Plans and Ordinances.* Washington, D.C.: Island Press, 1999.

Dargan, Mary Palmer, and Hugh Graham Dargan. *Timeless Landscape Design: The Four-Part Master Plan.* Layton, UT: Gibbs Smith, 2007. http://www.dargan.com/poppyshops

Dargan, Mary Palmer. *The Early English Kitchen Garden: 800 A.D. to 180 A.D.* Baton Rouge: LSU Press, 1981. http://www.dargan.com/poppyshops

Haque, Mary Taylor, Lolly Tai, and Don Ham. *Landscape Design for Energy Efficiency.* Clemson University, 2000.

McHarg, Ian. *Design with Nature* (Wiley Series in Sustainable Design). New York: 1969.

McQueen, Mike, and Ed McMahon. *Land Conservation Financing.* The Conservation Fund, 2003.

Environmental Philosophy

Louv, Richard. *Last Child in the Woods: Saving Our Children From Nature-Deficit Disorder.* New York: Algonquin Books, 2005.

Osler, Mirabel. *A Gentle Plea for Chaos.* New York: Arcade Publishing, 1989.

Stein, Sara. *Noah's Garden: Restoring the Ecology of Our Own Backyards.* New York: Houghton Mifflin Company, 1993.

Thompson, J. William, and Kim Sorvig. *Sustainable Landscape Construction: A Guide to Green Building Outdoors.* Washington D.C.: J. Island Press, 2000.

Vogel, A. *Nature: Your Guide to Healthy Living.* Druckerei und Verlagsanstalt Konstaz GmbH, 1986.

Lifestyle Patterns, Longevity and Elder Living

Buettner, Dan. *The Blue Zones: Lessons on Living Longer from the People Who've Lived the Longest.* National Geographic, 2008.

Center for Sustainable Economy: http://www.sustainable-economy.org/index.html

Elder Housing Trends. Cambridge Silver Ribbon Committee 2011. http://www.cambridgema.gov.

Kephart, Horris. *Camping and Woodcraft: A Handbook for Vacation Campers and Travelling in Wilderness.* Knoxville: University of Tennessee Press, 1998.

Mother Jones News: http://www.motherjones.com

US Census Bureau: http://www.census.gov/population

Gardening Philosophy

Church, Thomas D. *Gardens Are for People.* New York: Reinhold Publishing, 1955.

Eddison, Sydney. *Gardening for a Lifetime: How to Garden Wiser as You Grow Older.* Portland, OR: Timber Press, 2010.

Frederick, Jr., William H. *The Exuberant Garden and the Controlling Hand.* New York: Little, Brown and Company, 1992.

Jackson, John Brinckerhoff. *The Necessity for Runs, and Other Topics.* Amherst: The University of Massachusetts Press, 1980.

Karson, Robin. *Fletcher Steele, Landscape Architect: An Account of a Gardenmaker's Life, 1885–1971.* New York: Abrams/Sagapress, 1989.

Lawrence, Elizabeth. *A Garden of One's Own.* University Press, 1977.

Lufkin, Elise. *Not Bartlett's: Thoughts on the Pleasures of Life, People, Love, Gardens, Dogs, and More.* New York: Helen Marx Books, 2007.

Moore, Charles W., William J. Mitchell, and William Turnbull, Jr. *The Poetics of Gardens.* Cambridge: Massachusetts Institute of Technology Press, 1988.

Mosko, ASLA, Martin Hakubai, and Alxe Noden. *Landscape as Spirit: Creating a Contemplative Garden.* Weatherhill, 2003.

Norberg-Schultz, Christian. *Genius Loci: Towards a Phenomenology of Architecture.* New York: Rizzoli International Publications, Inc. 1984.

Pollan, Michael. *Second Nature: A Gardener's Education.* Delta, 1991.

Strong, Roy. *The Laskett: The Story of a Garden.* New York: Bantam Books, 2003.

Van Sweden, James. *The Artful Garden: Creative Inspiration for Landscape Design.* New York: Random House, 2011.

———. *Gardening with Nature.* New York: Watson-Guptill Publications, 2003.

Gardening Practices

Bartley, Jennifer. *Designing the New Kitchen Garden.* Portland, OR: Timber Press, 2008.

———. *The Kitchen Garden's Handbook.* Portland, OR: Timber Press, 2010.

Burrell, C. Colton. *Native Alternatives to Invasive Plants* (BBG Guides for a Greener Planet). Brooklyn, NY: Brooklyn Botanic Garden, 2006.

Cox, Jeff. *Your Organic Garden.* Emmaus, PA: Rodale Press, 1994.

Guinness, Bunny, and Jacqueline Knox. *Garden Your Way to Health and Fitness.* Portland, OR: Timber Press, 2008.

Neal, Nellie. *Organic Gardening Down South.* B. B. Mackey Books, 2008.

Ogden, Scott, and Lauren Springer. *Plants with Presence (Plant Driven Design: Creating Gardens that Honor Plants, Place, and Spirit).* Portland, OR: Timber Press, 2008.

Ondra, Nancy J., and Cohen, Stephanie. *The Perennial Gardener's Design Primer: The Essential Guide to Creating Simply Sensational Gardens.* North Adams, MA: Storey Publishing, 2005.

Oudolf, Piet, and Noel Kingsbury. *Designing with Plants.* Portland, OR: Timber Press, 1999.

———. *Planting Design: Gardens in Time and Space.* Portland, OR: Timber Press, 2005.

———. *Landscapes in Landscapes.* New York: Monacelli Press, 2010.

Raven, Sarah. *The Great Vegetable Plot.* BBC Books, 2008.

———. *Grow Your Own Cut Flowers.* Sarah Raven. BBC Books, 2008.

Robinson, William. *The Wild Garden.* Originally published in England in 1881. Portland, OR: Timber Press, reprinted in 1994.

Summers, Carolyn. *Designing Gardens with Flora of the American East.* New Brunswick, NJ: Rutgers University Press, 2010.

Yepsen, Roger. *Organic Plant Protection: A Comprehensive Reference on Controlling Insects and Diseases in the Garden, Orchard, and Yard—Without Chemicals.* Emmaus, PA: Rodale Press, 1976.

Smart House Planning and Design

LEED—www.usgbc.org

Susanka, Sarah. *The Not So Big House.* Taunton, 1998.

Courses and Societies

American Horticulture Therapy Association: http://www.ahta.org

Landscape Your Life: Create a Utopia in 5 easy steps: http://www.dargan.com/landscapeyourlife

Master Gardeners: http://www.ahs.org/mastergardeners

Index